Quiet Los Angeles

Quiet Los Angeles

Rebecca Razo

photographs by Mark Mendez
series editor Siobhan Wall

 FRANCES
LINCOLN

Frances Lincoln Limited
74–77 White Lion Street
London N1 9PF

Quiet Los Angeles

Text by Rebecca Razo
Photographs by © Mark Mendez, except:

p.8: © Diane Runyeon, courtesy The Bissell House Bed & Breakfast; p.12: © The Huntington Library, Art Collections, and Botanical Garden, photo by Tim Street-Porter; p.14, 15: Courtesy J. Paul Getty Trust; p.16: © Museum of Contemporary Art, photo by Marissa Roth; p.18: © Norton Simon Art Foundation, photo by Elon Schoenholz; p.21: Courtesy Griffith Observatory; p.26: © L.A. Law Library; p.29 (left): Photo by Noe Montes, courtesy Doheny Library; p.30: © The Huntington Library, Art Collections, and Botanical Garden; p.31: Photo by John Elder, courtesy Skirball Cultural Center; p.46: © Descano Gardens; p.51: Photo by David Wakely Photography, courtesy The Rancho Los Alamitos; p.52: Courtesy of the Earl Burns Japanese Garden photo archive; p.53: Photo by Austin Eguia, courtesy Gusdorf Marketing Group for South Coast Botanic Garden; p.55: Courtesy Mildred E. Mathias Botanical Collection; p.56: Photo by Tim Street-Porter, courtesy the Blue Ribbon Garden at the Walt Disney Concert Hall; p.57: © The Huntington Library, Art Collections, and Botanical Garden; p.65: © Catalina Island Chamber of Commerce (www.catalinachamber.com); p.74: Photo by Jaime Zapata, courtesy St. John's Episcopal Cathedral; p.86: Courtesy Hotel Casa del Mar; p.100: Photo by Nicholas Roberts, courtesy Café Gratitude; p.112: Courtesy TOMS; p.116: Courtesy Wayfarers Chapel; p.124: Photo by Nic Ray, courtesy Hollywood Forever Cemetery; p.136: The Langham Huntington Pasadena; p.138: Photo by Dan Duran, courtesy Topanga Canyon Inn Bed & Breakfast; p.139: The Beverly Hills Hotel, Dorchester Collection, Beverly Hills; p.140: © Diane Runyeon, courtesy The Bissell House Bed & Breakfast; p.141: Hotel Bel-Air, Dorchester Collection, Los Angeles; p.142: Photo by Bruce Royer, courtesy Tuscali Mountain Inn Luxury Bed & Breakfast; p.143: Courtesy Terranea Resort.

First Frances Lincoln edition 2016

978-0-7112-3690-5

Printed and bound in China

1 2 3 4 5 6 7 8 9

COVER Echo Park Lake BACK COVER El Matador State Beach
p.1 The Last Bookstore; p.2 Manhattan Beach Botanical Garden; OPPOSITE Rancho Palos Verdes; p.6 Abalone Cove Shoreline Park; p.8 The Bissell House Bed & Breakfast; p.9 Peace Awareness Labyrinth and Garden; p.10 Annenberg Gallery inside Los Angeles Public Library, Central Branch

Contents

Introduction

If I could add a Facebook relationship status for each of my favorite American cities, it would look something like this: Seattle—Married; New York—Engaged; Boston—In a relationship; Los Angeles—It's complicated. For the past 20 years, the City of Los Angeles and I have been in and out of love. Or, rather, I have been in and out of love with it. As it stands now, I'm back to being deeply enamored of the urban complex that represented the dreams of my youth. And it looks like it's going to stay that way.

For nearly a decade, back in what seems like an eternity ago, I was an officer with the Los Angeles Police Department. When I started my career in law enforcement, I was young and idealistic. And for a while, I loved my job and the City I served. But day after day, as I came into contact with the darker side of the human condition, the shine of my idealism began to tarnish and my affection for the City began to cool. I questioned whether my chosen vocation was right for me. Ultimately, I decided it wasn't and I left my career to forge a new path better suited to my personality. But leaving the Department meant that the City was no longer a fixture in my daily life—I live 40 miles away in another county. So along with my departure from the LAPD was the breakup of my relationship with the City that I so loved. It pained me.

When the opportunity to write *Quiet Los Angeles* came along, I didn't have to think twice. I not only looked forward to becoming reacquainted with the City of Angels, but I was excited at the prospect of discovering it anew—to see it not as a bleary urban

jungle, but rather as a haven capable of offering quiet respite, comfort, and even tranquility.

Over the next several months, as I walked around downtown and through Venice, Echo Park, Silverlake, Los Feliz, and Hollywood, I once again reveled in the magic of the City's cultural diversity, myriad topographies, and eclectic neighborhoods. The love affair was back on. But the romance didn't end there. I knew that I couldn't do this book justice by limiting my exploration to LA City proper. After all, when people think of Los Angeles, what they are really thinking of is the 4,750 square miles that make up the whole of Los Angeles County. And within the county are another 87 incorporated cities, including Long Beach, Rancho Palos Verdes, Pasadena, Santa Monica,

Manhattan Beach, San Pedro, and dozens of other districts and towns—all with distinct characteristics of their own—that compose the greater collective Los Angeles.

But where is one to find quiet in these heavily congested urban areas? There are, of course, places that naturally lend themselves to stillness: libraries (page 26); houses of worship (page 68); museums (page 12); parks (page 36); nature preserves, trails, and coastal areas (page 58). Driving is still the best method of transportation throughout Los Angeles, and there are miles and miles of peaceful scenic highways to enjoy (page 130). But the real fun is uncovering quiet, reposeful environments in unexpected places.

Take Urban Americana in Long Beach. Located in a 16,000-square-foot warehouse, this antique and design cooperative carries loads of unique items one would be hard-pressed to find in a small-town antiques mall. The space is large, but its relaxed atmosphere makes it a worthwhile spot to while away a few nostalgic hours looking through the treasures of yesteryear (page 115). Just a few blocks over is The Library (page 96), a coffee house where dark jewel-toned colors add a slightly gothic vibe, along with comfy velvet-upholstered sofas, tufted chairs, and mood lighting. It's a great place to grab a java—the Mexican mocha is especially good—and spend some time immersed in a 'borrowed' book. Over in the coastal Belmont Shore neighborhood, Lisa Ramelow, owner of La Strada Italiano (page 96), welcomes guests with a cheerful greeting and a friendly smile. You may want to nab one of the small tables on the tiny outdoor patio to do a bit of people watching or opt for an even cozier table inside. After your meal, take a walk through the tranquil and charming neighborhood streets just south of the restaurant over to the Belmont Pier near Termino Avenue and Ocean Boulevard. This lovely pier boasts a stunning view, especially at night when the air is cool and the location is—you guessed it—quiet.

The City of Los Angeles may be the hub of the entertainment industry, and the guy seated next to you at Fix Coffee (page 99) might very well be writing the next Academy Award-winning screenplay, but it actually takes work to find Hollywood pretense in the City's quietest haunts. In fact, most Angelenos eschew the phony veneer and are friendly, engaging, and approachable—even if they do bump elbows with celebrities. Harvey Jason and Louis M. Jason, owners of Mystery Pier Books in West Hollywood (page 83), are two such examples. Their cozy shop is tucked behind a building off the legendary Sunset Strip. They deal in rare books and boast an impressive celebrity clientele— Bono and Johnny Depp are regulars—but they're never too busy to chat with visitors about the one-of-a-kind literary works that line the shelves in this booklover's Shangri-La.

The Peace Awareness Labyrinth & Gardens (page 92) in South LA is about as far from the Hollywood scene

as you can get, even though its location, a c. 1910 Italian Renaissance Beaux-Arts mansion, once belonged to director Busby Berkeley. Today the serene meditation gardens and outdoor labyrinth, which was inspired by the labyrinth at Chartres Cathedral in France, encourages visitors to find spiritual balance.

A quiet garden art installation at the USC Fisher Museum of Art (page 23) encourages contemplation of an historical nature. Blacklist consists of ten stone benches and paved walkways engraved with quotes from the 'Hollywood Ten': ten filmmakers who were imprisoned and banned from working in Hollywood for refusing to testify in front of the House Un-American Activities Committee during the Cold War.

And then there are the little nooks and crannies that you won't find anywhere else but Los Angeles—like the 'secret' stairs. Scattered around the area's many hilly neighborhoods, these 'hidden' historic stairways are remnants from the City's streetcar and trolley era. There are more than 400 in the City; I've included just three (pages 123, 125, and 129).

An individual recently told me that he didn't 'get' LA because it 'has no real center,' like London or New York. But that's precisely what makes Los Angeles so special: it doesn't have one center; it has many. And within each of those centers are many more captivating quiet little spots, amid other surprises, just waiting to be discovered. To be sure, LA is multifaceted—even complex at times—but it always has something new it wants to reveal. In that, its mysteries are as intriguing as they are enchanting—more than enough to sustain a lifetime love affair filled with quiet exploration and peaceful escape in the City of Angels.

A note about the freeways, bus routes, and rail lines included in the text:
While I tried to include as accurate and comprehensive travel information as possible, space limitations prevented me from including every potential option. I therefore tried to include only the routes and/or lines that put commuters as close to the destination as possible. Please consult individual transit authority websites for connections and the most current information:
Los Angeles Metro Rail and Metro Bus: www.metro.net
City of Los Angeles Department of Transportation:
    www.ladottransit.com
Long Beach Transit: www.lbtransit.com
Big Blue Bus (Santa Monica Transit): www.bigbluebus.com
Palos Verdes Peninsula Transit Authority:
    www.palosverdes.com/pvtransit
Metro Link: www.metrolinktrains.com

Introduction

The *Annenberg Gallery* displays some of the extraordinary materials collected by the *Los Angeles Public Library* since its founding in 1872. The exhibit will rotate items selected from the library's collections including some from the special collections in the Rare Books Department. Hollywood—perhaps the most famous part of Los Angeles—is our featured collection.

Museums and galleries

The Huntington Library, Art Collections, and Botanical Gardens

1151 Oxford Rd., San Marino 91108 ☎ (626) 405-2100
$ (free for members and children under 4)
www.huntington.org
Open Monday, Wednesday–Friday 12pm–4.30pm, Saturday,
Sunday 10.30am–4.30pm (summer hours: 10.30am–4.30pm)
Parking Free
Freeway I-210, I-605, CA-134 **Bus** 78/79/378 (Metro Bus)
Metro Rail Gold line 804 to Allen Station (connection via
bus or taxi)
Buildings are wheelchair accessible

American and European paintings, prints, tapestries,
drawings, sculpture, and *objets d'art* come together in the
exquisite collections at The Huntington. While the works
cover periods from the 15th to the mid-20th century, two
perennial favorites that draw visitors from around the world
include Thomas Lawrence's *Sarah Barrett Moulton: Pinkie*
(c. 1794) and Thomas Gainsborough's *The Blue Boy* (c. 1770).
Other artists of note across the collections include Mary
Cassatt, Edward Hopper, William Blake, Albrecht Dürer, and
Rembrandt. After a walk through the exhibits, take some time
to enjoy freshly brewed tea, finger sandwiches, scones, and
a selection of desserts at the elegant Rose Garden Tea Room
(advance reservations required) or at one of the other cafés or
teahouses on the grounds.

The J. Paul Getty Museum (the Getty Center)

1200 Getty Center Dr. via N. Sepulveda Blvd., LA 90049 ☎ (310) 440-7300
Free www.getty.edu **Open** Tuesday–Friday, Sunday 10am–5.30pm, Saturday 10am–9pm, closed Monday
Parking Paid lot **Freeway** I-405 **Bus** 2, 234, 734 (Metro Bus); Big Blue Bus Route 14 (Santa Monica)
Metro Rail Expo line 806 to Culver City (connection via bus or taxi)
The center is wheelchair accessible

20th-century American oil tycoon Jean Paul Getty was an avid art collector. His passion for art inspired him to establish a museum in which to share his personal collection with the public. When Getty passed away in 1976, he bequeathed his fortune to the museum in trust. The endowment enabled the expansion of Getty's ideals through the formation of a foundation; research and conservation institutes; publications; and the J. Paul Getty Museum, composed of two separate locations: the Getty Center and the Getty Villa. The Getty Center is home to hundreds of works, including centuries-old antiquities, paintings, drawings, sculpture, and decorative arts. Magnificent gardens and grounds include quiet hideaways, fountains, lush lawns, and walkways, in addition to outdoor terraces with panoramic views of the city and the ocean.

The J. Paul Getty Museum (the Getty Villa)
17985 Pacific Coast Highway, Pacific Palisades 90272 ☎ (310) 440-7300
Free (advance entrance tickets are required) www.getty.edu
Open Wednesday–Monday 10am–5pm, closed Tuesday **Parking** Paid lot **Freeway** I-10, I-405
Bus 534 (Metro Bus) **Metro Rail** Expo line 806 to Culver City (connection via bus or taxi)
The museum is wheelchair accessible

Inspired by the Villa dei Papiri in Herculaneum, Italy, the Getty Villa features a permanent collection made up of Greek, Roman, and Etruscan antiquities dating from 6,500 B.C. to 500 A.D. Approximately 1,200 works from the collection's 44,000 pieces are on exhibit at any given time in 23 gallery spaces divided by theme. Sculpture, coins, jewelry, and other unique artifacts provide a glimpse into daily life hundreds of thousands of years ago, while another five galleries are dedicated to loans and traveling exhibitions from museums around the world. Outside the Villa, tranquil gardens, fountains, ponds, and footpaths include plenty of quiet resting spots, where visitors can take in the splendor of this location inspired by the ancient world.

The Museum of Contemporary Art, Grand Avenue

250 S. Grand Ave., LA 90012 ☎ (213) 621-1741
$ (free for children under 12) www.moca.org **Open** Monday, Wednesday, Friday 11am–6pm, Thursday 11am–8pm, Saturday, Sunday 11am–5pm, closed Tuesday **Parking** Paid lots, metered street parking **Freeway** US-101, I-10, I/CA-110 **Bus** 14/37, 70, 71, 76, 78/79/378, 96, 487/489, 707, 770, 910 (Metro Bus), DASH A, B (LADOT) **Metro Rail** Red line 802 to Pershing Square
All locations are all wheelchair accessible

With three separate locations in the city, postmodern art habitués will have no trouble feeding their obsession at the Museum of Contemporary Art, Los Angeles, where the works of Roy Lichtenstein, Mark Rothko, Robert Rauschenberg, Jackson Pollock, and dozens of other celebrated and emerging artists are on view. Installation, post-minimalism, pop art, and neo-expressionism are just a few of the genres from 1940 to the present expressed through painting, drawing, photography, sculpture, and other media. MOCA Grand Avenue consists of dozens of galleries, a café, and the flagship MOCA Store; The Geffen Contemporary at MOCA (152 N. Central Ave., LA) boasts 40,000 square feet of exhibit space, and MOCA Pacific Design Center (8687 Melrose Ave., W. Hollywood) rotates architecture and design exhibits.

The G2 Gallery

1503 Abbot Kinney Blvd., Venice 90291
☎ (310) 452-2842
Free www.theg2gallery.com
Open Monday–Saturday 10am–7pm,
Sunday 10am–6pm
Parking Metered street parking
Freeway I-10, I-405, CA-90
Bus 33, 733 (Metro Bus); Big Blue Bus
Route 2 (Santa Monica)
Metro Rail Expo line 806 to Culver City
(connection via bus or taxi)
The gallery is wheelchair accessible

Representing the works of numerous
celebrated artists, including Ansel Adams,
this award-winning gallery of nature and
wildlife photography is more than just a place
to view beautiful art. Founded in 2008 by
photographers and conservation advocates,
Dan and Susan Gottlieb, all proceeds generated
from art sales are donated to environmental
groups. The gallery exhibits are located on the
second level of the space and depict a range
of majestic scenes, from the awe-inspiring to
the mysterious. On the ground floor, the G2
Mercantile carries an eclectic assortment of
wares crafted by North American artisans.

Norton Simon Museum

411 W. Colorado Blvd., Pasadena 91105 ☎ (626) 449-6840
$ (free for students and children 17 and under) www.nortonsimon.org
Open Monday, Wednesday, Thursday, 12pm–5pm, Friday, Saturday 11am–8pm, Sunday 11am–5pm, closed Tuesday
Parking Free in lot **Freeway** I-210, I-605, CA-134 **Bus** 10, 180/181, 256, 780 (Metro Bus)
Metro Rail Gold line 804 to Del Mar
The museum is wheelchair accessible

20th-century entrepreneur Norton Simon was a passionate advocate of the arts. Containing works assembled from his private collection, this beautiful light-filled space is home to an extraordinary compendium of South and Southeast Asian art, as well as thousands of significant works of European art from the Renaissance to the 20th century. Rembrandt's *Portrait of a Boy* (c. 1655–60), van Gogh's *The Mulberry Tree* (c. 1889), and Picasso's *Woman with a Book* (c. 1932) are among these masterpieces, in addition to more than 100 works across a range of media by Edgar Degas—one of Simon's favorite artists. Visitors especially won't want to miss the Degas ballerina sculptures, which are truly mesmerizing.

Natural History Museum of Los Angeles County

900 Exposition Blvd., LA 90007 ☎ (213) 763-3466
$ (free for members) www.nhm.org
Open Sunday–Saturday 9.30am–5pm
Parking Paid lot
Freeway I-10, I/CA-110
Bus 81, 102, 200, 204, 442, 550 (Metro Bus),
DASH F, Southeast (LADOT)
Metro Rail Expo line 806 to Expo Park/USC
The museum is wheelchair accessible

Nature and culture intersect in this museum of wonder, learning, and discovery, which houses an astounding 35 million objects and artifacts in dozens of permanent exhibits and research collections. With so much to see, it might be hard to decide where to spend your time. Start with the original c. 1913 museum building, which merits a visit for its beautiful architectural details, including Italian marble, Corinthian pillars, mosaic-tile floors, and a coffered-ceiling rotunda with stained-glass dome. Just below, a rhythmical Beaux-Arts bronze sculpture depicts three outward-facing supernal figures standing in a circle and balancing a luminous sphere in hands raised gracefully above their heads; these 'Three Muses' represent the studies of art, history, and science. Outside, pretty gardens include an urban water feature, a pond, and a living wall wildlife habitat, in addition to walking paths and plenty of areas to sit.

LA Louver Gallery

45 N. Venice Blvd., Venice 90291 ☎ (310) 822-4955 **Free**
www.lalouver.com **Open** Check website, as hours change
Parking Paid lot across the street (free with gallery
validation) **Freeway** I-10, I-405, CA-90 **Bus** 33 (Metro Bus);
1 (Culver City) **Metro Rail** Expo line 806 to Culver City
(connection via bus or taxi)
The gallery is wheelchair accessible

The LA Louver Gallery has a long and distinguished list
of featured local and international artists. The serene
minimalist space contains two exhibition floors that
are open to the public, as well as a courtyard for show
openings and a unique skyroom for rotating exhibits.

Hammer Museum

10899 Wilshire Blvd., LA 90024 ☎ (310) 443-7000
Free www.hammer.ucla.edu **Open** Tuesday–Friday
11am–8pm, Saturday, Sunday 11am–5pm, closed Monday
Parking Paid lot, metered street parking **Freeway** I-405
Bus 6, 6R, 20, 234, (Metro Bus); Big Blue Bus Route 1,
2, 3M, 8, 12 (Santa Monica) **Metro Rail** Expo line 806 to
Culver City (connection via bus or taxi)
The museum is wheelchair accessible

The Hammer Museum maintains four onsite art collections
that include European and American works spanning the
centuries. A quiet courtyard café inside treats guests to
locally sourced seasonal fare in a relaxed setting.

Griffith Observatory

2800 E. Observatory Rd., LA 90027 ☎ (213) 473-0800
Free www.griffithobservatory.org **Open** Tuesday–Friday 12pm–10pm, Saturday, Sunday 10am–10pm, closed Monday
Parking Free in lot **Freeway** I-5, US-101 **Bus** 204 (Metro Bus); DASH Weekend Observatory Shuttle from
Vermont/Sunset Station (LADOT, Sat/Sun only) **Metro Rail** Red line 802 to Vermont/Sunset
The observatory is wheelchair accessible

You might recognize Griffith Observatory from the 1955 film, *Rebel Without a Cause,* or dozens of other movies and TV
shows that have been filmed there. More than a just scenic backdrop, however, the Observatory has been a unique
center for the exploration of the cosmos since it opened in 1935. Numerous exhibits, educational installations, a
planetarium, and Sunset Walk & Talk hikes are among the many things to see and do. The Observatory's rooftop terrace
is a lovely quiet spot to enjoy views of the city and the Hollywood sign; however, if you're looking to the sky for inspiration,
make sure to attend one of the free Public Star Parties, where visitors may view the moon, planets, and stars from
telescopes set up on the lawn. Experienced demonstrators manage the telescopes and are happy to answer questions.

Museum of Latin American Art

628 Alamitos Ave., Long Beach 90802 ☎ (562) 437-1689
$ (free for members, children under 12, and every Sunday) www.molaa.org
Open Wednesday, Thursday, Saturday, Sunday 11am–5pm, Friday 11am–9pm, closed Monday, Tuesday
Parking Free in lot **Freeway** I-405, I-710 **Bus** 71, 72, 91, 92, 93, 94 (Long Beach)
Metro Rail Blue line 801 to 5th Street
The museum is wheelchair accessible

Now celebrating its 20th anniversary, MOLAA curates exhibits and collections dedicated to contemporary Latin American art and culture. More than 1,300 works by artists from 20 Latin American countries make up its permanent collection, while a sculpture garden exhibits abstract and figurative works crafted from bronze, metal, steel, and wood. The café's courtyard patio is a pleasant, relaxing way to start—or end—your museum visit. Enchiladas, tacos, mole, chorizo, and other flavorsome Latin American dishes top the menu at Café Viva, in addition to beer, wine, Mexican coffee, and deserts.

USC Fisher Museum of Art

823 Exposition Blvd., LA 90089 ☎ (213) 740-4561
Free fisher.usc.edu
Open Tuesday–Friday 12pm–5pm, Saturday 12pm–4pm,
closed during holidays and summer months
Parking Paid lot **Freeway** I-10, I/CA-110 **Bus** 81, 102, 200,
204, 442, 550 (Metro Bus), DASH F, Southeast (LADOT)
Metro Rail Expo line 806 to Expo Park/USC
The museum is wheelchair accesible

Blacklist, perhaps the most compelling exhibit at this
impressive museum, sits outside in a quiet little garden.
The powerful installation represents the ominous
McCarthy Era in America during the Cold War.

University Art Museum, California State University Long Beach

1250 Bellflower Blvd., Long Beach 90840 ☎ (562) 985-5761
Free www.csulb.edu/org/uam
Open Check website as opening hours are subject to
change **Parking** Paid lot **Freeway** I-405, CA-22W
Bus 91, 92, 93, 94, 121, 171 (Long Beach)
Metro Rail Blue line 801 to Pacific Coast Hwy
The museum is wheelchair accesible

Contemporary visual art exhibits at this distinguished
museum seek to engage visitors for a thought-provoking,
meaningful, and compelling experience.

Long Beach Museum of Art

2300 E. Ocean Blvd., Long Beach 90803 ☎ (562) 439-2119
$ (free for members, children under 12) www.lbma.org
Open Thursday 11am–8pm, Friday–Sunday 11am–5pm
Parking Free street parking **Freeway** I-405, I-710
Bus 21, 22, 121 (Long Beach) **Metro Rail** Blue line 801 to Downtown Long Beach
The museum is wheelchair accessible

Beautifully landscaped gardens and lawns, two floors of gallery space, a restaurant and outdoor café, and views of the Long Beach Harbor and the Pacific Ocean make this quiet community museum a lovely place to spend a relaxing afternoon. Included in its permanent collection are English Staffordshire figurative earthenware ceramics from the 17th–19th centuries, in addition to a diverse assortment of late-20th-century ceramics. Rotating exhibits, from the classic to the contemporary, cover a range of mediums, including drawing, painting, glass, ceramics, textiles, metals, and wood—ensuring there is always something new and interesting on display.

California African American Museum
600 State Dr., Exposition Park, LA 90037 ☎ (213) 744-7432
Free www.caamuseum.org **Open** Tuesday–Saturday 10am–5pm, Sunday 11am–5pm
Parking Paid lot **Freeway** I-10, I/CA-110 **Bus** 81, 102, 200, 204, 442, 550 (Metro Bus), DASH F, Southeast (LADOT)
Metro Rail Expo line 806 to Expo Park/USC
The museum is wheelchair accessible

African American history and culture are beautifully revealed through this museum's diverse exhibits. Permanent collections include modern and contemporary art of the Harlem Renaissance and the emerging African Diaspora; traditional African art, including wood sculpture and masks; photographs and artifacts that speak to African American history and heritage; and insightful academic and naturalistic landscape paintings from the 19th century. An onsite non-lending research library, also open for public education and enjoyment, features more than 4,000 books across a number of subject areas; highlights include Antebellum Southern Plantations records from the American Revolution through the Civil War and a c. 1855 edition of *My Bondage and My Freedom* by Frederick Douglass.

Libraries and cultural centers

LA Law Library

301 W. 1st St., LA 90012 ☎ (213) 785-2529
Free www.lalawlibrary.org
Open Monday–Friday 8.30am–6pm, Saturday 9am–5pm
Parking Paid lots, metered street parking
Freeway I-10, I/CA-110, US-101
Bus 70, 71, 76, 78/79/378, 96, 487/489, 707 (Metro Bus/LADOT)
Metro Rail Red line 802 / Purple line 805 to Civic Center/
Grand Park
The library is wheelchair accessible

LA Law Library curates an inclusive collection of legal
encyclopedias, appellate briefs, law reviews, and data from
the 50 states and around the world. While certain areas are
reserved for legal professionals, the main floor is open to the
public for research and quiet study, with access to most of
the library's materials. This community resource is 'aimed
at promoting legal research and equal access to justice
throughout Los Angeles County.' Free classes and events are
ongoing and open to the public.

Los Angeles Public Library, Lincoln Heights Branch

2530 Workman Street, LA 90031 ☎ (323) 226-1692
Free www.lapl.org **Open** Monday, Wednesday 10am–8pm, Tuesday, Thursday 12pm–8pm,
Friday, Saturday 9.30am–5.30pm, closed Sunday
Freeway I-5, I/CA-110 **Bus** 28, 83, 251 (Metro Bus), DASH Lincoln Heights/Chinatown (LADOT)
Metro Link San Bernardino line to Cal State LA Metrolink Station
The library is wheelchair accessible

This branch of the Los Angeles Public Library was established in 1916 with funds made available through millionaire and philanthropist Andrew Carnegie's public library grants program. Inspired by the 16th-century Villa Papa Giulio in Rome, the Italian Renaissance building features a semi-circular design with high windows that run its length, an arched front entrance, a prominent multi-paned window, and a shingle-style roof. Also known as *Biblioteca del Pueblo de Lincoln Heights,* the branch is the second oldest in Los Angeles; it is listed as a Historic-Cultural Monument and on the National Register of Historic Places.

Doheny Memorial Library (USC)

3550 Trousdale Parkway, LA 90089 ☎ (213) 740-2924 **Free**
libraries.usc.edu/locations/doheny-memorial-library
Open Check website **Parking** Paid in lot
Freeway I-10, I/CA-110 **Bus** DASH F, Southeast (LADOT),
81, 102, 200, 204, 442, 550 (Metro Bus)
Metro Rail Expo line 806 to Expo Park/USC
The library is wheelchair accessible

Boasting hundreds of thousands of books, periodicals,
journals, manuscripts, and artifacts of historical
significance, this beautiful, Gothic-inspired, four-story
library on the USC campus is an educational and cultural
institution for students, faculty, and the community.

Santa Monica Public Library

601 Santa Monica Blvd., Santa Monica 90401 ☎ (310) 458-8600
Free smpl.org **Open** Monday–Thursday 10am–9pm, Friday,
Saturday 10am–5.30pm, Sunday 1pm–5pm **Parking** Paid
lot, metered street parking **Freeway** I-10, I-405 **Bus** 4, 704
(Metro Bus),Big Blue Bus Routes 1, 7, 8, 10 (Santa Monica)
Metro Rail Expo line 806 to Culver City (connection required)
The library is wheelchair accessible

This contemporary eco-conscious library has been
serving residents of the surrounding communities since
it opened in 2006. The history of the Santa Monica Public
Library, however, dates to 1876. Today the library offers
free computer classes and a variety of special programs.

The Huntington Library, Art Collections, and Botanical Gardens

1151 Oxford Rd., San Marino 91108 ☎ (626) 405-2100
$ www.huntington.org **Open** Monday, Wednesday–Friday 12pm–4.30pm, Saturday, Sunday 10.30am–4.30pm, closed Tuesday (summer hours: 10.30am–4.30pm) **Parking** Free **Freeway** I-210, I-605, CA-134 **Bus** 78/79/378 (Metro Bus)
Metro Rail Gold line 804 to Allen Station (connection via bus or taxi)
All buildings and most gardens areas are wheelchair accessible

The Huntington curates a collection of more than nine million rare books, manuscripts, photographs, and other materials related to British and American history, literature, science, and technology. Direct access to the reading rooms is not open to the general public; however, qualified academic faculty, librarians, curators, doctoral candidates, and independent scholars may request admittance via a formal application process. While the general public may not have access to these exclusive rooms, visitors will relish The Huntington's permanent and rotating exhibits in its galleries. Books and manuscripts from the Middle Ages to the present day offer an up-close look at significant works, including Chaucer's *Canterbury Tales,* the Gutenberg Bible, Shakespeare's First Folio, and works and letters from Louis Pasteur, Isaac Newton, Albert Einstein, Galileo, and others.

Skirball Cultural Center

2701 N. Sepulveda Blvd., LA 90049 ☎ (310) 440-4500
$ www.skirball.org **Open** Tuesday–Friday 12pm–5pm, Saturday–Sunday 10am–5pm, closed Mondays and holidays
Parking Free in lot; street parking is prohibited
Freeway I-405 **Bus** 234 (Metro Bus)
The center is wheelchair accessible

Galleries, exhibitions, educational programs, and performances are just some of the ways the Skirball Cultural Center endeavors to preserve and promote Jewish heritage and tradition, while celebrating multicultural diversity and inclusivity. Docent-led tours of the core exhibit, *Visions and Values: Jewish Life from Antiquity to America,* enlighten visitors about the historic and cultural relevance of the Judaica and Jewish art and artifacts in a collection of more than 25,000 objects. Outside, the Rainbow Arbor mist fountain, a lily pond, gardens, and numerous courtyards with tables and chairs, offer several peaceful spots to enjoy a snack from the grab-and-go food cart; alternatively, Zeidler's Café serves up flavorful lunches in a relaxed California-style bistro setting.

Beverly Hills Public Library

444 N. Rexford Dr., Beverly Hills 90210 ☎ (310) 288-2200 **Free**
www.beverlyhills.org/exploring/beverlyhillspubliclibrary
Open Monday–Thursday 9.30am–9.30pm, Friday, Saturday
10am–6pm, Sunday 12pm–6pm **Parking** Paid lot
Freeway I-405 **Bus** 4, 14/37, 16/36, 704 (Metro Bus)
Metro Rail Red line 802 to Vermont/Beverly (connection
via bus or taxi)
The library is wheelchair accessible

In addition to its extensive selection of books, reference
materials, and digital resources, this modern library
features an adjacent coffee shop, complementary Wi-Fi,
and a reading room reserved for quiet study.

The Markaz Arts Center
for the Greater Middle East

5998 W. Pico Blvd., LA 90035 ☎ (310) 657-5511 **Free**
www.themarkaz.org **Open** Monday–Friday 10am–6pm;
check website for events schedule **Parking** Metered street
parking **Freeway** I-10, I-405 **Bus** 105, 217 (Metro Bus) Big
Blue Bus Route 7 (Santa Monica Transit) **Metro Rail** Purple
line 805 to Western/Wilshire (connection via bus or taxi)
The building is wheelchair accessible

With an eye toward promoting interfaith unity and cross-
cultural understanding, this non-partisan center supports
community members with Mideast origins and beyond
through exhibitions, cultural events, and educational programs.

Los Angeles Public Library, Central Branch

630 W. 5th Street, LA 90071 ☎ (213) 228-7000
Free www.lapl.org
Open Monday–Thursday 10am–8pm, Friday,
Saturday 9.30am–5.30pm, Sunday 1pm–5pm
Freeway I-10, I/CA-110, US-101
Bus 16/316, 148, 53, 55/202/355, 62, 720 (Metro
Bus), DASH A, B, F (LADOT)
Metro Rail Red line 802/Purple line 805 to
Pershing Square or 7th Street/Metro Center, Blue
line 801/Expo line 806 to 7th Street/Metro Center
The library is wheelchair accessible

There are so many wonderful, interesting
things to see at the LA Public Library's Central
Branch, visitors can easily spend an entire day
taking in the beautiful art, architecture, and
design details throughout its quiet halls and
galleries. There is something of note on each
of the eight levels—even the elevator cars are
decorated with vintage index cards from the
Library's old catalog. The third largest central
library in the country, the Central Branch
houses 2.6 million books and 10,000 periodical
subscriptions, among millions more historic
and reference items. Be sure to take some
time in the breathtaking rotunda, where multi-
paned windows illuminate oil-painted murals,
exquisite mosaics, and the inimitable bronze
Zodiac Chandelier, all of which must be viewed
in person to be entirely appreciated.

West Hollywood Library

625 N. San Vicente Blvd., W. Hollywood 90069
☎ (310) 652-5340 **Free**
Open Monday–Thursday 11am–7pm, Friday,
Saturday 10am–6pm, closed Sunday
Parking Paid lot (3 hours free w/ library
validation) **Freeway** US-101
Bus 4, 30/330, 105, 305, 550, 705 (Metro Bus)
Metro Rail Red line 802 to Beverly/Vermont
(connection via bus or taxi)
The library is wheelchair accessible

This sustainably-designed library has numerous
quiet areas for reading, studying, and enjoying
views of the Hollywood Hills and the Pacific
Design Center from floor-to-ceiling glass
windows. A lovely sycamore tree art installation
reaches up from the wall of the central stairwell
to the skylight, while the handcrafted bamboo
ceiling, with large graceful carvings of vines,
leaves, and petals, is a piece of art all its own.
On the ground floor, a coffee shop brews up
traditional and specialty javas, while the Friends
of the Library used bookshop invites browsers
to pick up a favorite title or two for just a few
dollars.

Powell Library (UCLA)

405 Hilgard Ave., LA 90095 ☎ (310) 825-1938
Free www.library.ucla.edu/powell
Open Check website, as hours change
Parking Paid lots **Freeway** I-405
Bus 2, 234 (Metro Bus); Big Blue Bus Routes 1, 2, 8, 12 (Santa Monica)
Metro Rail Expo line 806 to Culver City (connection via bus or taxi)
The library is wheelchair accessible

Built in 1929, the Powell Library was the second building constructed on the UCLA campus. Inspired by Italian Romanesque, Byzantine, Spanish, and Moorish designs, this architectural prize features arched windows and doorways, intricate exterior scrollwork, carved wood newel posts and balustrades, ornate mosaics and tile work, and a striking rotunda. The Main Reading Room on the second floor features an octagonal dome with an intricate ceiling design consisting of historic printers marks. A large space designed for quiet study, the room houses the library's thematically curated Community Collections. The light-filled Rose Gilbert Reading Room features fewer flourishes, but is another quiet space to enjoy; materials in this room include magazines, journals, and periodicals.

Parks and green spaces

Palm Beach Park

Golden Shore Ave., south of Shoreline Dr., Long Beach 90802
☎ (562) 570-1600
www.longbeach.gov/park
Open Daily sunrise to sunset
Parking Metered lot
Freeway I-405, I-710 **Bus** 121 (Long Beach)
Metro Rail Blue line 801 to Downtown Long Beach
Paved paths make this park wheelchair accessible

This unassuming waterfront park overlooking Queensway Bay is not as well known as Shoreline Aquatic Park, its busier neighbor across the way, making it a nice quiet location to spend time away from the crowd. A short walk along a paved pathway from the adjacent Golden Shores Marine Biological Preserve, this park caters to those who want to enjoy a book or do some writing undisturbed. Within view is the Queensway Bridge and just beyond it, the Queen Mary. If wetland ecology interests you, bring binoculars to survey the wildlife in the Preserve—waterfowl are frequent guests who help themselves to the marshland's fish. A chain-link fence around the sanctuary restricts direct access; however, those interested in learning about the regional habitats will appreciate the interpretative signs posted near the site.

Biddy Mason Park

behind Broadway Spring Center, 333 S. Spring St., LA 90013
Open Daily sunrise to sunset **Parking** Paid lots, metered
street parking **Freeway** I-10, I/CA-110, US-101
Bus 2, 4, 30/330, 40, 45, 745 (Metro Bus)
Metro Rail Red line 802/Purple line 805 to Pershing Square
The park is wheelchair accessible

A public art installation pays tribute to the life and legacy
of Bridget 'Biddy' Mason in this relaxing and serene urban
green space tucked into a courtyard. Born a slave in the
South, Mason eventually won her freedom in California
and went on to become a nurse, entrepreneur, and the
first African American woman to own land in Los Angeles.

La Bella Fontana di Napoli (Naples Fountain)

N. Ravenna Dr. and Corinthian Walk, Long Beach 90803
☎ (562) 570-3232 www.longbeach.gov/park
Open Daily sunrise to sunset
Parking Metered street parking **Freeway** I-405, CA-22W
Bus 121, 131 (Long Beach) **Metro Rail** Blue line 801 to
Pacific Coast Hwy (connection via bus or taxi)
The park is wheelchair accessible

The highlight of this small community park in the heart of
Naples is a lovely fountain surrounded by brick pathways,
benches, four grassy mounds, and neatly groomed hedges.
It is seldom overcrowded and is also within walking
distance of the Naples Canals and Naples Plaza Park.

Griffith Park

4730 Crystal Springs Dr., LA 90027 ☎ (323) 913-4688
www.laparks.org **Open** Daily 6am–10pm
Parking Free in lots **Freeway** I-5, CA-134, US-101
Bus 96 (Metro Bus) **Metro Link** Antelope Valley Line to
Glendale Metrolink (Metro Link)
Most recreational areas are wheelchair accessible

Comprised of more than 4,000 acres, this beloved parkland
has been an integral part of Los Angeles since philanthropist
Colonel Griffith J. Griffith bequeathed it to the community
more than a century ago. The beautiful hiking trails, quiet
resting spots, scenic peaks, and diverse vegetation and
wildlife, make for a peaceful outdoor experience.

Ernest E. Debs Regional Park (Debs Park)

4235 Monterey Rd., LA 90032 ☎ (213) 847-3989
www.laparks.org **Open** Daily sunrise to sunset
Parking Free in lots **Freeway** I-5, I/CA-110 **Bus** 252 (Metro
Bus) **Metro Rail** Gold line 804 to Southwest Museum
Most recreational areas are wheelchair accessible

Native shrubs and foliage support abundant wildlife in this
park, and visitors are sure to spot dozens of animals and
a variety of bird species. Visit the park's Audubon Center
for a comprehensive list of inhabitant wildlife to look for.
Numerous trails of varying degrees of difficulty lead to
stunning vistas of the Los Angeles Basin, downtown, and
the San Gabriel and San Bernardino Mountain ranges.

Will Rogers State Historic Park

1501 Will Rogers State Park Rd., LA 90272 ☎ (310) 454-8212
www.parks.ca.gov
Open Daily 8am–sunset **Parking** Paid lot **Freeway** I-10, I-405 **Bus** 2 (Metro Bus)
Metro Rail Expo line 806 to Culver City (connection via bus or taxi)
Some picnic areas are wheelchair accessible; access service available to Inspiration Loop Trail (call ahead); Ranch House is wheelchair accessible, though some slopes may require assistance

Will Rogers was one of Hollywood's most beloved movie stars of the 1920s–30s. In 1922, Rogers purchased nearly 200 acres of land and cultivated it into an authentic Western ranch and 31-room residence, where he lived with his family until his untimely death in 1935. A national and state historic monument, the park is an inclusive haven with hiking and riding trails, recreational areas, a visitor center, docent-led tours of the Ranch House (Thursday–Sunday), and self-guided tours of the expansive grounds. Don't miss the 2.25-mile hike to Inspiration Point for breathtaking panoramic views of the city and the Santa Monica Bay.

Barnsdall Art Park

4800 Hollywood Blvd. LA 90027 www.barnsdall.org
Open Daily 5am–10pm **Parking** Free in lots
Freeway US-101 **Bus** 180/181, 206, 217 (Metro Bus)
Metro Rail Red Line 802 to Vermont/Sunset
Location is wheelchair accessible; elevators at the south
end near Red Line exit and at base of Barnsdall Art Center

Dedicated to supporting the arts for public enrichment
and enjoyment, the 11 acres that compose Barnsdall Art
Park include the Barnsdall Art Center; Junior Art Center;
Los Angeles Municipal Art Gallery; Gallery Theatre;
and the Hollyhock House, Frank Lloyd Wright's first
architectural development in Los Angeles.

Elysian Park

835 Academy Rd., LA 90012 ☎ (213) 485-5054
www.laparks.org **Open** Daily 5am–9pm **Parking** Free in
lots **Freeway** I-5, I/CA-110, CA-2 **Bus** DASH Pico Union/
Echo Park (LADOT) **Metro Rail** Red line 802 to Beverly/
Vermont (connection via bus or taxi)
Most picnic and recreational areas are wheelchair accessible

Elysian Park consists of hilly woodland, trails, manicured
lawns, and recreational areas, segmented by paved winding
roads. Both Dodger Stadium and the original Los Angeles
Police Academy are located within the grounds. Among the
park's highlights is the Chavez Ravine Arboretum, founded in
1893, and declared a Historical Cultural Monument in 1967.

Spring Street Park
426 S. Spring St., LA 90013
friendsofspringstreetpark.com
Open Daily sunrise to sunset
Parking Paid lots, metered street parking **Freeway** I-10, I/CA-110, US-101
Bus 28, 40, 83 (Metro Bus) **Metro Rail** Red Line 802, Purple Line 805 to Pershing Square
The park is wheelchair accessible

A relatively new addition to downtown Los Angeles, this dog-friendly urban common is just under an acre
and offers respite from the hectic city beyond its enclosure. Among its features are an oval grassy knoll, brick
pathways, a fountain, numerous seating areas, and a separate children's play area. Bordered by drought-resistant
native vegetation and LED lighting, this aesthetically pleasing park creates an interesting juxtaposition of clean
contemporary design against the detailed architecture of the historic buildings surrounding it.

Point Vicente Interpretive Center / Point Vicente Lighthouse

31501 Palos Verdes Drive W., Rancho Palos Verdes 90275 ☎ (310) 377-5370
Open Park: daily sunrise to sunset
Interpretive Center: daily 10am–5pm
Lighthouse: 2nd Saturday of the month (except March) 10am–3pm, first Saturday of the month (except March) 10am–4pm
Parking Free in lot
Freeway I/CA-110
Bus 344 (Metro Bus); Orange, Gold, Blue Routes, Routes 225, 226 (Palos Verdes Peninsula Transit)
Metro Rail Green line 803 to Harbor Freeway station (connection via bus or taxi)
Interpretive Center and park are wheelchair accessible

Shade trees, grassy areas, picnic tables, and walking paths make up the landscape of this coastal park and educational facility. Exhibits in the Interpretive Center focus on the history of the Peninsula, with resources dedicated to educating the public about the Pacific gray whale, which can be viewed onsite during the mammal's annual migration from December to April. Directly adjacent to the park, the c. 1926 Point Vicente Lighthouse remains functional and shines its beam 185 feet above the ocean to help guide seafarers around the rocky coast. Legend has it the lighthouse is haunted by the 'Lady of the Light,' an otherworldly figure in a flowing gown who appears on the tower's walkway. Whether this essence is the ghost of the first lighthouse keeper's wife who fell to her death from a cliff, or a woman grieving her beloved lost at sea, the mythology endures as part of this location's history.

Hilltop Park

2351 Dawson Ave., Signal Hill 90755 ☎ (562) 989-7330
www.cityofsignalhill.org **Open** Daily sunrise to sunset
Parking Free street parking **Freeway** I-405 **Bus** 21, 22 (Long
Beach) **Metro Rail** Blue line 801 to Willow Street
The park is wheelchair accessible

This three-acre park at the top of Signal Hill offers
sweeping views of the Pacific Ocean, Long Beach, and
the LA Basin. Walking paths, picnic tables, and plenty
of grassy areas make it a wonderful spot to enjoy a lazy
afternoon. Outward-facing benches are perfect for taking
in the sunset and the nighttime sparkle of the city lights
below.

Echo Park Lake

751 Echo Park Ave., LA 90026 ☎ (213) 847-0929
Open Daily sunrise to sunset **Parking** Metered street
parking **Freeway** I/CA-110, US-101 **Bus** 92 (Metro Bus),
DASH Pico Union / Echo Park (LADOT) **Metro Rail** Red
line 802 to Vermont/Beverly (connection via bus or taxi)
Paved paths make this park wheelchair accessible

Just beyond the shadow of Dodger Stadium is Echo Park
Lake: a man-made reservoir surrounded by walking
paths, palm trees, and lotus flowers. Make sure to look
for The Lady of the Lake statue, a Depression-era Art
Deco treasure that spent years forgotten in a city storage
facility before it was restored and returned to the park.

Kenneth Hahn State Recreation Area

4100 S. La Cienega Blvd., LA 90056
☎ (323) 298-3660
www.parks.ca.gov
Open Daily 6am–sunset
Parking Free in lot **Freeway** I-10, I-405
Bus 102, 212 (Metro Bus) **Metro Rail** Expo line
806 to La Cienega/Jefferson
This park is not wheelchair accessible

Biking, horseback riding, serene walking paths, and miles of hiking trails are among the offerings of this recreational getaway bursting in native coastal vegetation and wildlife. On a clear day, the park offers views of the San Gabriel Mountains rising spectacularly behind the downtown skyline. A fishing lake, lotus pond, and Japanese garden, in addition to picnic tables and a self-guided exercise course, make this an inclusive outdoor designation to enjoy a range of relaxing activities. Gray fox, desert cottontail, and California quail are among the wildlife visitors might spy while taking in the surroundings along the park's myriad footpaths.

Gardens

Descanso Gardens

1418 Descanso Dr., La Cañada Flintridge 91011
☎ (818) 949-4200
$ (free for members and children under 5)
www.descansogardens.org
Open Daily 9am–5pm
Parking Free in lot
Freeway I-210, CA-2 **Bus** 3, 32, 33 (Glendale)
Metro Link Antelope Valley Line to Glendale Metrolink (Metro Link) (requires connection via bus or taxi)
Most of the grounds are wheelchair accessible

Whether you'd prefer to linger in the aromas of roses and lilacs, observe the majesty of centuries-old oak trees, learn to create a sustainable garden, or discover a bit of regional history, this beautiful place at the foot of the Angeles National Forest will not disappoint. Footpaths and nature trails weave their way around grounds that include a large grassy common, as well as a Japanese garden, oak forest, a lake, and other beautiful flora. In 1937, E. Manchester Boddy, owner of the *Los Angeles Daily News,* purchased the Descanso land and commissioned 'architect to the stars,' James E. Dolena, to build a 22-room mansion for his family. Two decades later, Boddy sold the property to the county and volunteers began transforming it into the impressive gardens they are today. To fully appreciate the history and heritage of this spot, make sure to tour the Boddy House, which is open 10am to 4pm, Tuesday through Sunday. And for a truly mesmerizing experience, pay a visit during the RISE of the Jack o' Lanterns in the evenings during the months of October and November.

Exposition Park Rose Garden

at Exposition Park, 701 State Drive, LA 90037 ☎ (213) 765-5397
Free www.laparks.org
Open Daily 9am–sunset (Garden is closed yearly from January–March 15 for pruning)
Parking Paid lot **Freeway** I-10, I/CA-110 **Bus** DASH F, Southeast (LADOT), 35, 81, 102, 200 (Metro Bus)
Metro Rail Expo line 806 to Expo Park/USC
Paved paths make the perimeter wheelchair accessible; however, the garden itself consists of landscaped grass, making it a challenge to navigate

This pleasing garden brims with roses of every imaginable size, shape, and color. Neatly arranged beds of Whisper, Dynasty, Granada, Timeless, Kaleidoscope, and hundreds of other varietals stretch across beautifully manicured lawns permeating the air with a cornucopia of delightful fragrances. Gazebos and benches offer numerous areas in which to sit quietly and enjoy the garden's large central fountain, for a pleasant getaway in the middle of the city.

James Irvine Japanese Garden

at the Japanese American Cultural &
Community Center, 244 S. San Pedro St.,
LA 90012 ☎ (213) 628-2725
Free www.jaccc.org
Open Tuesday–Friday 10am–5pm; call ahead
for weekend hours (schedule subject to change
without notice), closed Monday
Parking Paid lots, metered street parking
Freeway I-10, I/CA-110, US-101
Bus DASH A, D (LADOT) **Metro Rail** Gold line
804 to Little Tokyo/Arts District
The immediate entrance to the garden is paved,
making it wheelchair accessible

Accessible through the Japanese American
Cultural & Community Center, this *Seiryu-en*,
or 'Garden of the Clear Stream,' is a tranquil
hideaway in downtown's Little Tokyo district.
Dozens of trees, flowers, plants, and grasses
are interspersed between large and small rock
formations, cedar bridges, curving footpaths,
and a gently flowing brook. This garden isn't
large and won't take long to walk through;
however, it's a divine spot to enjoy an afternoon
break. Make sure to check out JACCC's events
calendar, as well as the George J. Doizaki
Gallery, which mounts changing art exhibits
throughout the year that speak to Japanese and
Asian culture.

Maguire Gardens

on the grounds of Los Angeles Central Library
accessible from Flower St. south of 5th St.
630 W. 5th St., LA 90071
☎ (213) 228-7000 **Free**
Open Daily sunrise to sunset
Parking 524 S. Flower St. Garage (paid lot;
reduced rate w/ library validation), metered
street parking
Freeway I-10, I/CA-110, US-101
Bus 16/316, 148, 53, 55/202/355, 62, 720 (Metro
Bus), DASH A, B, F (LADOT)
Metro Rail Red line 802/Purple line 805 to
Pershing Square or 7th Street/Metro Center, Blue
line 801/Expo line 806 to 7th Street/Metro Center
The park is wheelchair accessible

Were it not for the shimmer of the Westin
Bonaventure Hotel towering above, it would be
easy to forget that this little garden is located
in the middle of a lively city center. Located
just behind the LA Central Library, a split-
level terraced walkway flanks three shallow
reflecting pools adjacent to the casual yet
elegant California-French bistro, Café Pinot.
Olive and jacaranda trees provide shade across
beautifully manicured lawns dotted with public
art installations, benches, and fountains. On a
clear day, this outdoor space is ideal for relaxing
with a sack lunch and a book.

The Rancho Los Alamitos

6400 Bixby Hill Rd., Long Beach 90815 ☎ (562) 431-3541
Free www.rancholosalamitos.com **Open** Wednesday–Sunday 1pm–5pm
Parking Free in lot **Freeway** I-405, I-605, I-710 **Bus** Long Beach Transit 81 (Mon–Fri), 91/94 (Sat/Sun)
Metro Rail Blue Line 801 to Willow St. (connection via bus or taxi)
Majority is wheelchair accessible; some narrow paths may not be accessible

The rich and storied history of Rancho Los Alamitos dates back to 500 A.D. when it was the sacred land of California's Gabrielino-Tongva Indian tribe. Over the centuries that followed, the property was bought, sold, and changed hands many times. During the 19th and 20th centuries the Rancho began shaping local commerce in the fields of farming, ranching, oil, and real estate. It's been home to generations of people and a source of steady employment for many more. It was also significant to the formation of the City of Long Beach. In 1968, the property's last remaining heirs donated the ranch and the land to the city. Today it is a Southern California cultural destination consisting of an historic Ranch house, four acres of gardens, several other historic structures and landscapes, and an educational center and bookstore.

Earl Burns Miller Japanese Garden

1250 Bellflower Blvd., Long Beach 90840 ☎ (562) 958-8885
Free www.csulb.edu/jgarden **Open** Tuesday–Friday 8am–3pm, Sunday 12pm–4pm, closed Monday, Saturday, and during campus winter recess **Parking** Metered lot **Freeway** I-405, CA-22W **Bus** 91, 94, 121, 171 (Long Beach)
Metro Rail Blue Line 801 to Willow St. (connection via bus or taxi)
The garden is wheelchair accessible

A gift from Lorraine Miller Collins in honor of her late husband, Earl Burns Miller, this serene one-acre Japanese garden on the campus of Long Beach State University was designed to complement and enrich the education of students and the community. Upon entering, visitors are treated to an exquisite variety of textures, including bamboo, stone, rock, wood, and metal, intermingled with the gifts of nature. Bonsai, juniper, ginkgo, birch, hydrangea, azalea, camellia, and weeping willow are just some of the flora that shares subtle fragrances throughout the striking landscapes. Traditional Japanese symbolic statuary adds to this meaningful experience, while The Moon Bridge, Tea House Room, Dry Garden Room, Zig-Zag Bridge, koi pond, and gently flowing waters invite myriad opportunities for quiet contemplation.

South Coast Botanic Garden

26300 Crenshaw Blvd., Rancho Palos Verdes 90274 ☎ (310) 544-1948
$ (free 3rd Tuesday of the month, for members, and children 4 and under) southcoastbotanicgarden.org
Open Daily 9am–5pm **Parking** Free in lot **Freeway** I/CA-110 **Bus** Green Route, Route 226 (Palos Verdes Peninsula
Transit) **Metro Rail** Green line 803 to Harbor Freeway station (connection via bus or taxi)
Accessibility generally limited to the immediate 10 acres around the administration buildings

More than 2,500 plant and flower species from North America, Australia, Africa, South America, and the Mediterranean, make up this expansive 87-acre garden. Nicknamed 'the Jewel of the Peninsula' for its coastal geography, the garden was cultivated over what was once a sanitary landfill, demonstrating the art of land reclamation at its finest. Dozens of footpaths wind their way through more than 35 collections, including areas devoted to dahlias, grasses, fuchsia, juniper, magnolia, redwood, palm, ficus, and desert vegetation. To get the most from their experience, visitors are encouraged to smell and touch the plants and flowers. Fountains, arbors, bridges, and waterways complement the already dazzling surroundings, while plenty of benches and seating areas are available for brief respites.

Manhattan Beach Botanical Garden

1236 N. Peck Ave., Manhattan Beach 90266
☎ (310) 546-1354
Free www.manhattanbeachbotanicalgarden.org
Open Daily sunrise to sunset
Parking Free street parking
Freeway I-405 **Bus** 126 (Metro Bus)
Metro Rail Green line 803 to Redondo Beach
(connection via bus or taxi)
Paved paths make location wheelchair
accessible, although there are several inclines

Founded more than 20 years ago by local
citizens to address issues of changing
biodiversity, as well as to educate the public
about wildlife and conservation, this teaching
garden in the South Bay features a number of
unique topographies. Trees, wildflowers, lilacs,
sages, currants, grasses, gooseberries, and
succulents are among its native vegetation. The
garden is small, but it packs a lot in: a bird and
butterfly habitat, children's discovery garden,
a meditation garden, wildflower meadow,
interpretive signs, plant identification labels,
and a covered amphitheater are but a few of
its sceneries. After your visit, enjoy a picnic or
some additional quiet time by the lake at the
adjacent Polliwog Park.

Mildred E. Mathias Botanical Garden (UCLA)

777 Tiverton Dr., LA 90095 ☎ (310) 825-1260
Free www.botgard.ucla.edu
Open Monday–Friday 8am–5pm, Saturday, Sunday 8am–4pm, closed during university holidays
Parking Paid lots, metered street parking **Freeway** I-405 **Bus** 2 (Metro Bus); Big Blue Bus Routes 1, 2, 8, 12 (Santa Monica) **Metro Rail** Expo line 806 to Culver City (connection via bus or taxi)
Wheelchair-accessible paths run through the west side of the garden

An award-winning pioneer in the field of botanical research, horticulture, and ethnopharmacology, Dr. Mildred E. Mathias was a passionate advocate of conservation and an outspoken opponent of the destruction of the world's tropical rainforests. Mathias joined UCLA in 1944 as an herbarium botanist. She continued to grow into more prominent positions, including director of UCLA's Botanical Garden, until her retirement in 1974. Today the garden is an educational resource for students and the community. It includes pretty footpaths that loop around Hawaiian, Californian, and Australian natives; Malesian Rhododendrons; cycad, lily, fern, palm, and bromeliad gardens; and a bird and butterfly habitat.

The Blue Ribbon Garden at the Walt Disney Concert Hall

111 S. Grand Ave., LA 90012 ☎ (213) 972-7211
Free www.musiccenter.org/about/Our-Venues/
Our-Outdoor-Venues
Open Before and after performances, and daily
during normal business hours
Parking Paid lot, metered street parking
Freeway I-10, I/CA-110, US-101
Bus 14/37 (Metro Bus), DASH A, B (LADOT)
Metro Rail Red/Purple line to Civic Center/
Grand Park
The location is wheelchair accessible

Still one of LA's best-kept secrets, and often
only discovered through word of mouth, the Walt
Disney Concert Hall, which was designed by
distinguished architect Frank Gehry, features
a gorgeous rooftop garden unseen from the
building's exterior. While the garden sometimes
hosts events, it is open daily to the public and
can be accessed via an elevator outside the
hall's main entrance or an outdoor staircase—
also well concealed—that wraps its way around
the building all the way to the top. (It's several
hundred steps, so not for the faint of heart!)
Beautiful trees, flowers, grasses, and shrubs
bloom year-round in this urban green space,
with stone paths that lead to a large rose-
themed fountain, crafted from broken pieces of
Delft porcelain.

The Huntington Library, Art Collections, and Botanical Gardens

1151 Oxford Rd., San Marino 91108 ☎ (626) 405-2100

$ (free for members, children under 4) www.huntington.org **Open** Monday, Wednesday–Friday 12pm–4.30pm, Saturday, Sunday 10.30am–4.30pm, closed Tuesday (summer hours: 10.30am–4.30pm) **Parking** Free **Freeway** I-210, I-605, CA-134 **Bus** 78/79/378 (Metro Bus) **Metro Rail** Gold line 804 to Allen Station (connection via bus or taxi)
All buildings and most gardens areas are wheelchair accessible

More than 15,000 varieties of plant make up The Huntington's Botanical Gardens. Magnificent marble, bronze, and limestone sculptures blend in beautifully with the surrounding blooms. Delight in the aromatic rose and camellia gardens, which exhibit more than 2,400 combined cultivars. The Australian, Herb, Jungle, Palm, Desert, and Ranch gardens impress in equal measure. If your time is limited, make sure to visit the Chinese and Japanese gardens, in addition to the enchanting Shakespeare garden where a bust of the bard celebrates his works—some of which are on view in The Huntington's Library building. Those wishing to stay up to date on horticultural science may enjoy the complimentary lectures held on the second Thursday of the month, while others may want to shop for rare plants at the annual Spring Plant and Fall Plant sales.

Beaches and trails

Leo Carrillo State Park and Beach

35000 Pacific Coast Hwy, Malibu 90265
☎ (310) 457-8143
www.parks.ca.gov
Open Daily 8am–10pm; Visitor Center: Friday,
Saturday 10am–2pm
Parking Paid lot
Freeway I-405, US-101 **Bus** 534 (Metro Bus)
Metro Rail No rail access
Location is wheelchair accessible; some assistance may be
required

Named for California conservationist and actor Leo Carrillo,
this park is known for its campgrounds sheltered by
sycamore trees, in addition to hiking trails, beach caves,
and reefs. Onlookers are often treated to an impromptu
performance of skillful windsurfers whose deft and graceful
command of the sea can be awe-inspiring. A visitor's center
offers nature walks and other outdoor programs during the
summer months, and park rangers are available to answer
questions for daytime visitors and overnight guests who stay
in one of the campsites.

Abalone Cove Shoreline Park & Beach

5970 Palos Verdes Dr. South, Rancho Palos Verdes 90275
☎ (310) 544-5260 www.pvplc.org/_lands/abalone_cove.asp
Open Monday–Friday 12pm–4pm, Saturday, Sunday
9am–4pm **Parking** Paid lot **Freeway** I/CA-110
Bus 344 (Metro Bus); Orange, Gold, Blue, 225, 226 (Palos
Verdes Peninsula Transit) **Metro Rail** Green line 803 to
Harbor Freeway station (connection via bus or taxi)
Parking and recreation areas are wheelchair accessible

Part of the Abalone Cove Ecological Reserve, this beautiful
coastal landscape includes walking paths amid native
wildflowers, trees, and shrubs, in addition to picnic areas
and out-of-the-way spots to enjoy the incredible views.

Pelican Cove Park

31300 Palos Verdes Dr. South, Rancho Palos Verdes 90275
☎ (310) 544-5260 www.rpvca.gov **Open** Daily one hour
before sunrise to one hour after sunset
Parking Free in lot **Freeway** I/CA-110 **Bus** 344 (Metro
Bus); Orange, Gold, Blue, 225, 226 (Palos Verdes
Peninsula Transit Authority) **Metro Rail** Green line 803 to
Harbor Freeway station (connection via bus or taxi)
Parking and recreation areas are wheelchair accessible

This picturesque seaside spot borders Terranea Bluff Top
Park with access to the Terranea Discover Trail, a marine
interpretive site with a small beach, caves, and tide pools.
A magnificent place to explore the Pacific Coast ecosystem.

Point Dume State Beach

7103 Westward Beach Rd., Malibu 90265 ☎ (310) 457-8143
www.parks.ca.gov
Open Daily sunrise to sunset
Parking Paid lot
Freeway I-405, US-101 **Bus** 534 (Metro Bus) **Metro Rail** No rail access
The beach is not wheelchair accessible

An isolated stretch of beach, tide pools, and an ancient coastal bluff sand dune are the highlights of this littoral sanctuary. A popular spot for swimmers, surfers, and scuba divers, locals know Point Dume as a peaceful hangout away from the more crowded beaches further down the coast. Portions of this expanse are protected as a nature preserve that is home to dozens of wildlife, including birds, sea stars, urchins, and crabs. Other critters that inhabit the rocky chasms are ground squirrels, rabbits, and lizards, whereas sea lions, harbor seals, and dolphins are often seen splashing through the foamy crest of the sea.

Will Rogers State Beach

17000 Pacific Coast Hwy, Pacific Palisades 90272
PCH & Temescal Canyon Rd. ☎ (310) 305-9503
www.parks.ca.gov
Open Daily sunrise to 10pm **Parking** Paid lot
Freeway I-405 **Bus** 534 (Metro Bus)
Metro Rail Expo line 806 to Culver City (connection via bus or taxi)
The beach is not wheelchair accessible

While this beach features a range of amenities, including volleyball courts and bike paths, it stays surprisingly free of heavy crowds, making it a pleasant spot to spend a low-key afternoon. During the day, sightseers will undoubtedly spot surfers, skin divers, and the occasional fisherman. In the evening, this beach is one of the best locations to watch as the sun tucks itself into the western horizon.

Malibu Lagoon State Beach

23200 Pacific Coast Hwy, Malibu 90265 ☎ (310) 457-8143
www.parks.ca.gov
Open Daily 8am–sunset
Parking Paid lot
Freeway I-405, US-101 **Bus** 534 (Metro Bus) **Metro Rail** No rail access
Some trails and exhibits are wheelchair accessible

As home to the legendary Surfrider Beach, one might think that Malibu Lagoon would be constantly swarming with people. While the summer months can be busy, it's well worth a visit during the off-season to watch the morning surfers ride the waves like pros. Other activities include docent-led tours of the wetlands and bird watching, in addition to walking through the Malibu Lagoon Museum and the Adamson house, a c. 1929 Spanish Colonial Revival listed on the National Register of Historic Places, which educates visitors about the area's culture and history.

Cahuenga Peak

Wonder View Trail Head off Wonder View Dr.
Parking Free street parking on Lake Hollywood Dr.
(parking prohibited between 9pm–6am)
Freeway US-101 **Bus** 222 (Metro Bus) **Metro Rail** Red line
802 to Hollywood/Highland (connection via bus or taxi)
The trail is not wheelchair accessible

To access this challenging three-mile trail, head up
Barham Blvd north to Lake Hollywood Drive. Head east to
Wonder View Drive until it ends. Start the hike at Wonder
View Trail Head, commencing east on the Tree of Life Trail.
Follow the trail to Mount Lee, the summit that will take you
just behind the giant letters of the Hollywood sign.

Solstice Canyon Trail

Corral Canyon Rd. and Solstice Canyon Rd., Malibu 90265
☎ (805) 370-2301 (visitor's center) www.nps.gov
Open Daily 8am–sunset **Freeway** I-405 **Bus** 534 (Metro Bus)
Some parts of the trail are wheelchair accessible

Originally settled by the Chumash Indians thousands of
years ago, Solstice Canyon's unique history and landscape
makes it a site worthy of exploration. Nestled into the Santa
Monica Mountains, a year-round waterfall, streams, and
rock pools intermingle with native shrubs and chaparral
along an easily traversable trail. Remnants of noteworthy
buildings remain, including the foundations of lab buildings
where space-mission satellites were tested in the '60s and '70s.

Catalina Island
☎ (310) 510-1520
www.catalinachamber.com
The island can be reached by air (a 15-minute flight) or sea (an hour by boat), see website for details
Island is wheelchair accessible, although there are inclines

Located 22 miles off the Southern California coast, Catalina is quaint, charming, and—perhaps with the exception of the summer months—rarely overly congested. Perfect for a day trip or weekend getaway, the island's main town, Avalon, is just one square mile. Vehicle traffic is controlled so most get around by foot or on golf carts, which are available to rent. The island has many activities, including hiking and snorkeling; however, lots of people do little more than relax on the beach. For virtual solitude, take a jaunt to Two Harbors on the other side of the island. It's far less traveled than Avalon and has several quiet campgrounds, as well as limited accommodations. Transportation from the mainland is available by public and private aircraft, but most people catch one of the express ferries with daily departures out of Long Beach, San Pedro, Dana Point, and Newport Beach.

El Matador State Beach

32350 Pacific Coast Hwy, Malibu 90265
☎ (818) 880-0363
www.parks.ca.gov
Open Daily 8am–sunset
Parking Free in lot, but limited
Freeway I-405, US-101 **Bus** 534 (Metro Bus)
Metro Rail No rail access
The beach is not wheelchair accessible

Ten miles north of Malibu is El Matador, one of three pocket beaches that make up Robert H. Meyer Memorial State Beach. While celebrated by the locals, this Southern California gem isn't as well known to the general public, making it a lovely spot to enjoy some quiet time, particularly during the week when it is virtually empty. To access, visitors must descend a stairway 150 feet to the bottom. Sister beaches, El Pescador and La Piedra, are similarly situated and, like El Matador, offer solitude by the sea.

Portuguese Bend Reserve
Crenshaw Blvd. at Burrell Ln., Rancho Palos
Verdes 90275 ☎ (310) 541-7613
pvplc.org/_lands/portuguese_bend.asp
Open Daily sunrise to sunset
Parking Paid lot
Freeway I/CA-110 **Bus** 344 (Metro Bus); Blue,
225 (Palos Verdes Peninsula Transit)
Metro Rail Green line 803 to Harbor Freeway
station (connection via bus or taxi)
Parking and recreation areas are wheelchair
accessible

Dozens of trails weave their way through the
canyons and habitats of this nearly 400-acre
preserve overlooking the Pacific Ocean. Fragrant
wildflowers, native shrubs, and dozens of
unique rock formations are home to numerous
types of wildlife, including many sensitive
species. Adventurous hikers will like journeying
across multiple paths down and across Palos
Verdes Drive South, where they can access the
Inspiration Point vista and the tide pools, sea
caves, and black sands of Sacred Cove below.
Rocks in the cove can be slippery, and hiking
during high tide is strongly discouraged, as the
waters can be unexpectedly rough.

Places of worship

Church of the Good Shepherd

504 N. Roxbury Dr., Beverly Hills 90210 ☎ (310) 285-5425
www.goodshepherdbh.org
Open Check website for service and program times
Parking Free in lot, free street parking
Freeway I-405 **Bus** 4, 16/316 (Metro Bus)
Metro Rail Red line 802 / Purple line 805 to Wilshire/Vermont
(connection via bus or taxi)
The church is wheelchair accessible

Established in 1923, this Catholic parish has a long-standing
history in the Beverly Hills community, including a noteworthy
connection to the entertainment industry. With the dawning
of the Golden Age of Hollywood, the Church established the
Catholic Motion Picture Guild, which subsequently attracted
a number of celebrities to the flock, including Loretta Young,
Rosalind Russell, Irene Dunn, and others; even President John
F. Kennedy attended mass at the church on occasion. Today the
parish welcomes individuals of all backgrounds, and sponsors
a number of programs that encourage service to others. A
silent meditation group meets in the Parish Center Chapel
every Tuesday, Thursday, and Saturday.

Temple Emanuel Beverly Hills

8844 Burton Way, Beverly Hills 90211 ☎ (310) 288-3737
www.tebh.org **Open** Check website for worship and Shabbat service times
Parking Free in lot **Freeway** I-405 **Bus** 16/36 (Metro Bus)
Metro Rail Red line 802 to Vermont/Beverly (connection via bus or taxi)
The temple is wheelchair accessible

Founded in 1938, this modern Reform Jewish temple supports its members in their quest for a meaningful life by celebrating Jewish culture, tradition, and learning, alongside worship, social justice, community, and spirituality. Connection, inspiration, and 'a passion to repair the world' are among its creeds, while endeavoring to create an environment that is as open and encouraging as it is thought provoking. Built in 1951, the synagogue itself was one of the earliest to boast a contemporary design and was architect Sidney Eisenshtat's first large project of a house of worship. Eisenshtat, whose work has often been compared to that of Frank Lloyd Wright, went on to become one of the leading architects of modern-design synagogues and Jewish centers.

Westwood Methodist Church

10497 Wilshire Blvd., LA 90024 ☎ (310) 474-4511
www.westwoodumc.org **Open** Sunday Sanctuary service
and Sunday service in The LOFT at 10am **Parking** Free in
lot **Freeway** I-405 **Bus** 20 (Metro Bus) **Metro Rail** Expo line
806 to Culver City (connection via bus or taxi)
The church is wheelchair accessible

This church offers a warm refuge open to persons of all
backgrounds and beliefs. Two types of worship service—
one traditional, one contemporary—appeal to a broad
range of parishioners, while various ministries, including
mission work, a fair trade coffee program, and food pantry
are open to all who wish to participate.

Saint Monica Catholic Community

725 California Ave., Santa Monica 90403 ☎ (310) 566-1500
www.stmonica.net **Open** Monday–Friday 6.30am, 8am,
12.10pm; Saturday 8am, 5.30pm; Sunday 7.30am, 9.30am,
11.30am, 1.15pm, 5.30 pm **Parking** Free street parking,
limited church parking **Freeway** I-405 **Bus** Big Blue Bus
3M Route (Santa Monica) **Metro Rail** Expo line 806 to Culver
City (connection via bus or taxi)
The church is wheelchair accessible

Although the current Saint Monica church was built in 1925,
the parish dates back to 1886 when it was one of just a few in
the LA area. Inside the sanctuary, impressive classic columns
support arches that run the length of a barrel-vaulted ceiling.

Wilshire Boulevard Temple

3663 Wilshire Blvd., LA 90010 ☎ (213) 388-2401
www.wbtla.org **Open** Check website for worship and Shabbat service times
Parking Free in lot, metered street parking
Freeway I-10, US-101 **Bus** 20 (Metro Bus) **Metro Rail** Purple line 805 to Wilshire/Normandie
The temple is wheelchair accessible

This c. 1929 Byzantine-Revival temple was the third built for Congregation B'nai B'rith, LA's first Jewish synagogue founded in 1862. Listed on the National Register of Historic Places, the sanctuary features stunning stained-glass windows, black marble columns, gold inlay, intricately carved woodwork, ornate chandeliers, and beautifully crafted mosaics. Original painted murals, rendered by artist Hugo Ballin and commissioned by Warner Bros. studio chief Jack Warner, depict scenes of Biblical significance. In 1937, the congregation officially became Wilshire Boulevard Temple; today it operates multiple campuses and schools, offers dozens of services, and participates in a number of community outreach programs.

St Vincent de Paul Catholic Church

621 W. Adams Blvd., LA 90007
☎ (213) 749-8950
www.stvincentla.net
Open Check website for service and program
times **Parking** Free in lot
Freeway I/CA-110 **Bus** 14/37 (Metro Bus)
Metro Rail Expo line 806 to 23rd Street
The church is wheelchair accessible

St Vincent de Paul's heritage dates back to
1865 when it was St Vincent College, which
initially hosted mass in its chapel for a small
group of worshippers. Attendance flourished
over the next several decades, necessitating
a bigger space. Los Angeles oil magnate and
philanthropist Edward Doheny answered the
call to build a new worship center with a $1
million donation. The new Roman Catholic
parish—whose architectural design was
heavily influenced by the elaborate cathedrals
of Mexico—opened in 1925. Today the church
is a city historic-cultural monument and
remains one of the most striking buildings in
South Los Angeles. The sanctuary boasts gold
inlay, painted statuary, and intricately carved
woodwork, among other opulent details.

St John's Episcopal Cathedral

514 W. Adams Blvd., LA 90007 ☎ (213) 747-6285
www.stjohnsla.org
Open Check website for service and program times
Parking Free in lots
Freeway I/CA-110 **Bus** 14/37 (Metro Bus) **Metro Rail** Expo line 806 to 23rd Street
The cathedral is wheelchair accessible

This historic Episcopalian cathedral in South Los Angeles is home to the Bishop of the Diocese, J. Jon Bruno, and shares Diocesan functions with the Cathedral Center of St Paul in nearby Echo Park. The congregation was founded in 1890; however, its Romanesque edifice dates to 1924 and was inspired by the ancient Church of San Pietro in Tuscania, Italy. It is also listed on the National Register of Historic Places. A progressive and inclusive faith-based community, St John's welcomes people from all walks of life.

Cathedral of our Lady of the Angels

555 W. Temple St., LA 90012 ☎ (213) 680-5200
www.olacathedral.org
Open Check website for service times; guided
tours: Monday–Friday 1pm
Parking Paid lot for visitors; free validation with
mass attendance
Freeway I-10, I/CA-110, US-101
Bus 4 (LADOT) **Metro Rail** Red line 802/Purple
line 805 to Civic Center/Grand Park
The cathedral is wheelchair accessible

As home to the Los Angeles Archdiocese, this
grand cathedral is one of the city's distinguished
parishes. Its celebrated repute notwithstanding,
this holy gathering place is a true oasis in the
middle of the city. An outdoor plaza is open
daily and features dozens of areas to sit in quiet
thought. Fountains with Biblical significance,
meditation and olive gardens, art installations,
and a lovely café with open patio seating make
this a retreat for all to enjoy. Myriad themes
layered into the design details of the church's
exterior and light-filled sanctuary hold meaning
and value in relation to its doctrine.

Angelus Temple
1100 Glendale Blvd., LA 90026 ☎ (213) 816-1109
www.angelustemple.org / www.dreamcenter.org
Open Sunday 9.30am, 11.30am; Thursday 7pm
Parking Free in lot **Freeway** I/CA-110, US-101
Bus 92 (Metro Bus) **Metro Rail** Red line 802 to Vermont/Beverly (connection via bus or taxi)
The temple is wheelchair accessible

'Come as you are' is the refrain of Angelus Temple, where the evangelical Foursquare denomination originated in 1923 under minister Aimee Semple McPherson. In addition to carrying forward the legacy of the faith, today the church runs The Dream Center, an outreach facility dedicated to helping those impacted by a number of adverse life situations. While its congregation is large, the Church's small groups support individuals who desire to better understand and build their faith in close fellowship with others.

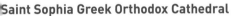

Saint Sophia Greek Orthodox Cathedral

1324 S. Normandie Ave., LA 90006 ☎ (323) 737-2424
www.stsophia.org **Open** Check website for service times;
cathedral visiting hours: Tuesday–Friday 10am–4pm,
Saturday 10am–2pm, Sunday 12.30pm–2pm
Parking Free in lot **Freeway** I-10, I/CA-110 **Bus** 206,
30/330 (Metro Bus) **Metro Rail** Red line 802/Purple line
805 to Wilshire/Vermont (connection via bus or taxi)
The cathedral is wheelchair accessible

Taking its influence from Hellenic and Byzantine traditions,
this awe-inspiring cathedral enjoys a number of impressive
architectural and design details. A painting of the Virgin Mary
with outstretched arms reminds us that all are welcome here.

Thien Hau Temple

750 N. Yale St., LA 90012 ☎ (213) 680-1860
www.thienhautemple.com **Open** Daily 8am–5pm
Parking Metered street parking **Freeway** I-10,
I/CA-110, US-101 **Bus** 81, 90/91, 94, 96 (Metro Bus)
Metro Rail Gold line 804 to Chinatown
The temple is wheelchair accessible

This grand Taoist temple in LA's Chinatown attracts the most
congregants in the months just before and after Chinese
New Year. At this time of celebration, individuals come to
worship, give thanks, and leave offerings on the altars.
Througout the rest of the year, the temple is a quiet place for
veneration, open to both worshippers and visitors of all faiths.

BOUGHT & SOLD
OLD & NEW
CURIOUS & RARE

BOOKS ARE
LASTING
GIFTS

PRINTS
FOR
SALE

UNCLE

CLEA
SA

UND

Bookshops

Caravan Book Store

550 S. Grand Ave., LA 90071 ☎ (213) 626-9944
Open Monday–Friday 11am–6pm, Saturday 12pm–5pm,
closed Sunday
Parking Metered street parking, paid lots
Freeway I-10, I/CA-110, US-101
Bus 14, 37, 70, 71, 76, 78, 79, 378 (Metro Bus)
Metro Rail Red line 802/ Purple line 805 to Pershing Square
The shop is wheelchair accessible

Founded in 1954 on what was then known as 'booksellers row',
this downtown bookshop, which specializes in rare and antique
titles, is a true city treasure. Owner Leonard Bernstein—whose
parents opened the store so they could be with each other every
day—recalls spending his youth in the shop wrapping packages,
sweeping floors, and learning the book business along the
way. This, Leonard notes, was back when Los Angeles still
ran streetcars and men and women wore neatly pressed suits
accessorized with hats and gloves. Leonard has run the store
now for more than four decades, and while the city outside has
changed dramatically, the inside of this little shop continues to
pay homage to the vintage books on its shelves and the stories
they keep.

Gatsby Books

5535 E. Spring St., Long Beach 90808 ☎ (562) 208-5862
www.gatsbybooks.com **Open** Monday–Thursday 10am–
6pm, Friday–Sunday 10am–5pm **Parking** Free in lot
Freeway I-405 **Bus** 91, 104 (Long Beach) **Metro Rail** Blue
Line 801 to Willow Street (connection via bus or taxi)
The shop is wheelchair accessible

Gatsby Books—the 'literary heart of Long Beach'—has
just about everything a booklover wants in an independent
bookshop: a knowledgeable, well-read owner; cool
T-shirts and tote bags; an aloof mascot cat named Ruby;
small-group book and poetry readings; and a diverse
selection of new and used titles.

Chevalier's Books

126 N. Larchmont Blvd., LA 90004 ☎ (323) 465-1334
www.chevaliersbooks.com **Open** Daily 10am–6pm
Parking Metered street parking **Freeway** US-101
Bus 14, 37 (Metro Bus) **Metro Rail** Red line 802 to
Vermont/Beverly (connection via bus or taxi)
The shop is wheelchair accessible

This bookshop has been a favorite literary stop in Larchmont
Village's Windsor Square for more than 75 years. Known for
its friendly staff and great customer service, the shop houses
a diverse selection of titles. A special area devoted to Los
Angeles celebrates local artists, designers, and architects, as
well as the cultural diversity and history of the city itself.

Traveler's Bookcase

8375 W. 3rd St., LA 90048 ☎ (323) 655-0575
www.travelersbookcase.com
Open Monday 11am–7pm, Tuesday–Friday 10.15am–7pm, Saturday 10am–7pm, Sunday 12pm–6pm
Parking Free in lot **Freeway** I-10 **Bus** 16, 218, 316 (Metro Bus)
Metro Rail Purple line 805 to Wilshire/Western (connection via bus or taxi)
The shop is wheelchair accessible

For a magical book-browsing experience, look no further than this whimsical, welcoming travel bookshop destined to spark curiosity and wanderlust. Well-traveled, friendly staff are prepared to make recommendations on books covering every latitude and longitude, while a range of cookbooks comprising a variety of international cuisines will tempt even those who don't know a sauté pan from a skillet. A colorful children's section encourages learning and cultural diversity, while practical foreign-language and geographic guidebooks and travel accessories will help trekkers plan their escape, whether crossing the border or crossing the ocean.

Harmony Fine Books and Art

at Counterpoint Records & Books
5911 Franklin Ave., Hollywood 90028
☎ (323) 957-7965
www.counterpointla.com
Open Harmony: Wednesday–Friday 12pm–8pm,
Saturday 12pm–6pm, Sunday–Tuesday by
appointment. Counterpoint: daily 11am–11pm
Parking Metered street parking
Freeway US-101 **Bus** 180, 181, 217 (Metro Bus);
DASH Hollywood (LADOT)
Metro Rail Red line 802 to Hollywood/Western
Both shops are small and may be difficult to
navigate in a wheelchair

Now celebrating its third decade in business,
this shop in Hollywood's Franklin Village
sells new, used, and rare books across art,
literature, film, and theater, as well as an
eclectic selection of vinyl; however, it's the
Harmony Fine Books and Art annex next door
where bibliophiles can spend hours of quiet
time perusing everything from signed playbills
and hard-to-find literary journals to poetry
chapbooks. Expert staff are happy to make
recommendations or just talk shop.

Mystery Pier Books

8826 Sunset Blvd., West Hollywood 90069 ☎ (310) 657-5557
www.mysterypierbooks.com **Open** Monday–Saturday 11am–
7pm, Sunday 12pm–5pm **Parking** Metered street parking
Freeway US-101 **Bus** 2 (Metro Bus) **Metro Rail** Red line 802
to Hollywood/Highland (connection via bus or taxi)
The shop is not wheelchair accessible

Blink and you might miss the corridor that leads to one of
the most unique bookshops in LA. Located on the Sunset
Strip, this purveyor of rare, first edition, and antiquarian
books boasts an impressive clientele and more impressive
collection. Its greatest attribute is the cordiality of owners,
father and son Harvey and Louis M. Jason.

Mystic Journey Bookstore

1624 Abbot Kinney Blvd., Venice 90291 ☎ (310) 399-7070
www.mysticjourneybookstore.com **Open** Sunday–
Thursday 11am–9pm, Friday, Saturday 11am–11pm
Parking Metered street parking **Freeway** I-10, I-405,
CA-90 **Bus** 33, 733 (Metro Bus) **Metro Rail** Expo line 806
to Culver City (connection via bus or taxi)
The shop is wheelchair accessible

Mystic Journey is a one-stop shop for spiritual growth and
mindfulness. In addition to a wide-range of metaphysical
and wellness titles, its offerings include crystals, incense,
herbs, essential oils, body care products, and yoga gear.
The outdoor courtyard provides a quiet space for browsing.

The Last Bookstore

453 S. Spring St., LA 90013 ☎ (213) 488-0599
www.lastbookstorela.com **Open** Monday–Thursday 10am–10pm, Friday, Saturday 10am–11pm, Sunday 10am–9pm
Parking Metered street parking, paid lots **Freeway** I-10, I/CA-110, US-101 **Bus** 28, 40, 83 (Metro Bus)
Metro Rail Red/Purple Line to Pershing Square
The bookstore is wheelchair accessible

The architecture alone is a worth an outing to the Spring Arts Tower: the exquisite Art Deco edifice that's home to The Last Bookstore in downtown's Historic Core. Constructed in 1915 by celebrated architects Parkinson and Bergstrom, the building's first anchor tenant was Citizens National Bank. Today hundreds of new and used books, vinyl records, and graphic novels fill the space amid installation art, a tunnel and pass-through assembled from books, color-coordinated stacks, and other unique eye candy. While the ground floor is frequently busy, the 'Labyrinth Above The Last Bookstore' on the mezzanine level contains a large, virtually silent back room brimming with $1 books. And don't miss the creepy but cool 'crime, law, horror, and weirdness' section inside one of the original bank vaults.

Book Soup

8818 Sunset Blvd., West Hollywood 90069 ☎ (310) 659-3110
www.booksoup.com **Open** Monday–Saturday 9am–10pm, Sunday 9am–7pm
Parking Metered street parking **Freeway** US-101
Bus 2 (Metro Bus) **Metro Rail** Red line 802 to Hollywood/Highland (connection via bus or taxi)
Newsstand and front of shop are wheelchair accessible

Floor-to-ceiling bookshelves are configured in an almost artistic arrangement in this unconventional haven of literature, known as the 'bookseller to the great & infamous'. In this shop, independent presses are celebrated alongside thousands upon thousands of art, film, photography, music, literary fiction, and avant-garde titles. Erudite staff are eager to recommend their picks, answer questions, and converse on the topics of the day, while a storefront newsstand features a breadth of reading material, including hard-to-find periodicals. Novelty gifts and cards are located at the front of the store. And don't be surprised if you look up to see a celebrity cruising down an aisle—though it's considered poor form to do anything other than nod, smile, and get on with your day.

Places to relax

Sea Wellness Spa

in Casa del Mar Hotel by the Sea
1910 Ocean Way, Santa Monica 90405 ☎ (310) 581-7767
www.hotelcasadelmar.com/wellness-spa-los-angeles
Open Sunday–Wednesday 9.30am–6pm,
Thursday–Saturday 8am–8pm
Parking Paid lot **Freeway** I-10, I-405, CA-90
Bus Big Blue Bus Routes 1, 7, 8, 20, 33 (Santa Monica)
Metro Rail Expo line 806 to Culver City (connection via
bus or taxi)
The spa is wheelchair accessible

Peace and tranquility await guests of the Sea Wellness Spa
located inside the Casa del Mar, an exquisite 1920s beachfront
hotel in fashionable Santa Monica. Inspired by the healing
properties of the ocean and designed using reclaimed wood
planks carefully recovered from a 19th-century Amish barn, this
eco-friendly spa offers a variety of services. Restorative anti-
aging facials and advanced skincare therapies, in addition to
body wraps, traditional Thai massage, and hot-stone and deep-
tissue massage are just a few of the treatments that help melt
away stress so guests leave feeling renewed and revitalized.
Extended services include private yoga and fitness sessions on
the beach with qualified trainers.

Tai Chi with Angie Sierra

In Point Fermin Park, directly across from
910 W. Paseo Del Mar, San Pedro 90731
www.angiesierra.com
Free (but donations welcome)
Open Saturday 9.45am
Parking Free street parking
Freeway I/CA-110 **Bus** 246 (Metro Bus)
Metro Rail Green line 803 to Harbor Freeway
station (connection via bus or taxi)
The park is wheelchair accessible

Life coach and spiritual mentor Angie Sierra
hosts free beginning Tai Chi classes in peaceful
outdoor surroundings around LA. The San Pedro
class, held on a small grassy bluff overlooking
the Pacific Ocean, starts with a gentle warm-
up, followed by the 24-form Yang Style Tai Chi:
meditative movements that promote a balance
of Yin and Yang energy. A silent three-minute
meditation rounds out the session to end.

Larchmont Sanctuary Spa

331 N. Larchmont Blvd., LA 90004
☎ (323) 466-1628
www.larchmontsanctuary.com
Open Wednesday–Monday by appointment,
closed Tuesday
Parking Free in lot, metered street parking
Freeway US-101 **Bus** 14, 37 (Metro Bus)
Metro Rail Red line 802 to Vermont/Beverly
(connection via bus or taxi)
The spa is wheelchair accessible

Tina Figueroa left a lucrative career in the tech
industry to open a day spa that would foster
connection in the community. Years of traveling
for work meant abundant opportunities for
Tina to experience treatments in some of the
world's most celebrated spas, which ultimately
helped her design a first-class menu for
her own boutique. Housed in a 100-year-old
bungalow, this spa offers a variety of exceptional
treatments to relax, refresh, and rejuvenate.
Organic facials, acupuncture, hydrotherapy,
and a range of bodywork treatments, including
Jade Stone massage, are among the offerings;
however, a Couples Champagne Bath in an
ergonomic copper tub has proven to be a client
favorite. Indoor and outdoor treatment rooms
add a unique touch, while a cozy common area
includes a fireplace, reading materials, berry-
infused waters, and healthy snacks.

Liberation Yoga

124 S. La Brea Ave., LA 90036
☎ (323) 964-5222
www.liberationyoga.com
Open Check website for class schedules
Parking Free in lot (limited), metered street parking
Freeway I-10 **Bus** 212, 312 (Metro Bus)
Metro Rail Red line 802 to Vermont/Beverly (connection via bus or taxi)
The studio is wheelchair accessible

Consistently ranked one of the top yoga studios in the city, Liberation Yoga encourages authentic living, spirituality, connection, and community through the practice of Hatha yoga. Owners Christine Burke and Gary McCleery believe that the transformative, healing powers of yoga and meditation not only contribute to an individual's physical health, inner peace, and serenity, but by extension add to the growth and betterment of the world at large. Classes range from beginning to advanced, while specialty classes cater to families, toddlers, pre- and post-natal women, and individuals in recovery and with Parkinson's. The studio also offers massage, Reiki, and advanced teacher-training workshops.

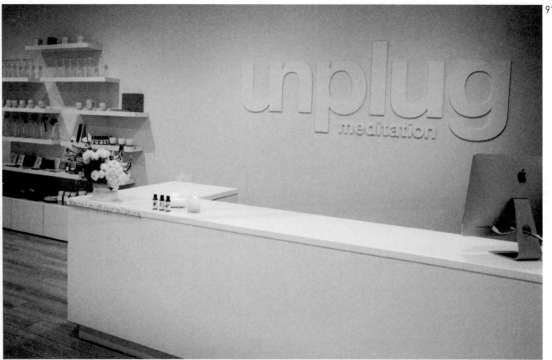

Unplug Meditation

12401 Wilshire Blvd., Suite 101, LA 90025 ☎ (310) 826-8899
www.unplugmeditation.com **Open** Check website for class schedules
Parking Paid lot, metered street parking
Freeway I-405 **Bus** Big Blue Bus Route 2 (Santa Monica), 20 (Metro Bus)
Metro Rail Expo line 806 to Culver City (connection via bus or taxi)
The studio is wheelchair accessible

Unplug Meditation's goal is simple: to change the world one breath at a time. Owner Suze Yalof Schwartz opened
Unplug to cater to individuals on the go—people with busy lives who want to power down from the daily grind to reclaim
a sense of calm and balance. Experienced, inspirational instructors lead 30- and 45-minute guided-meditation classes
inside a soothing, minimalist studio. Traditional and specialized classes cover basic meditation practices, breath work,
tapping, and silent mantra repetition, among others. Family and children's classes are also available, and many of the
team's instructors host events, workshops, and retreats.

Peace Awareness Labyrinth & Gardens

3500 W. Adams Blvd., LA 90018
☎ (323) 737-4055
www.peacelabyrinth.org
Free (entrance tickets required)
Open Hours subject to change without notice; please call ahead
Parking Free in gated lot, street parking
Freeway I-10 **Bus** 14, 37 (Metro Bus)
Metro Rail Expo line 806 to Expo/Crenshaw station (connection via bus or taxi)
Main building/grounds are wheelchair accessible; labyrinth/gardens have many steps so not accessible

This c. 1910 Italian Renaissance Beaux-Arts mansion once belonging to Hollywood director Busby Berkeley is home to the Movement of Spiritual Inner Awareness and the Peace Theological Seminary & College of Philosophy. The tranquil meditation gardens on these secluded grounds offer refuge amid beautiful fountains, lily ponds, lush trees, and fragrant flowers. The outdoor labyrinth, inspired by the one at Chartres Cathedral in France, is crafted from hand-cut travertine marble and invites guests to be still for a moment in spiritual meditation.

Long Beach Meditation
741 Atlantic Ave., Long Beach 90813 ☎ (562) 606-0643
www.longbeachmeditation.com
Open Check website for class and retreat schedules
Parking Free in lot
Freeway I-405, I-710 **Bus** 61 (Long Beach) **Metro Rail** Blue line 801 to 5th Street
Meditation studio is on second floor, accessible via steps; accommodations will be made for those unable to access

Long Beach Meditation is a non-profit organization dedicated to furthering the understanding and art of meditation in a safe and nurturing environment. An inclusive studio that welcomes individuals of all faiths and belief systems, the center practices Vipassana meditation: 'a time-honored method for developing mindfulness and concentration.' In addition to weekly mediation sits, the center offers beginning, intermediate, and advance courses, as well as morning, daylong, and weekend retreats.

Restaurants, bars and cafés

Valerie Confections Tea House & Bakery

1665 Echo Park Ave., LA 90026 ☎ (213) 250-9365
www.valerieconfections.com
Open Monday–Thursday 8am–4pm, Friday, Saturday
8am–6pm, Sunday 9am–5pm
Parking Free street parking
Freeway CA-2, I/CA-110, US-101
Bus DASH Pico Union/Echo Park (LADOT)
Metro Rail Red line 802 to Vermont/Beverly (connection
via bus or taxi)
The café is wheelchair accessible

Valerie Confections was founded a little more than a decade
ago when it had just six flavors of chocolate-dipped toffee
to its credit. Today the award-winning chocolatier has three
city locations and an assortment of goodies that includes its
signature toffees, as well as truffles, cakes, cookies, pastries,
preserves, and more. Indeed, Valerie's Tea House & Bakery
in Echo Park is loved as much for its sweet treats as for its
palatable seasonal fare consisting of brunch entrees, salads,
tartines, sandwiches, and coffees and teas. Nestled into a
quiet residential neighborhood, this café on the corner invites
guests to stay awhile with its alfresco seating and an inviting
covered patio.

La Strada Italiano

4716 E. 2nd St., Long Beach 90803 ☎ (562) 433-8100
www.lastradalongbeach.com **Open** Daily 11.30am–10pm
Parking Paid lots, metered street parking **Freeway** I-405,
CA-22W **Bus** 121, 131 (Long Beach) **Metro Rail** Blue line 801
to Pacific Coast Hwy (connection via bus or taxi)
The restaurant is wheelchair accessible

A favorite Italian eatery in the coastal Belmont Shore
community, this small bistro is big on warmth and
hospitality. While low music occasionally plays in the
background, the walls and ceiling are furnished with
hidden sound proofing material to absorb excessive noise
and allow diners to enjoy conversation undisturbed.

The Library: A Coffee House

3418 E. Broadway, Long Beach 90803 ☎ (562) 433-2393
www.thelibraryacoffeehouse.com **Parking** Metered and
free street parking **Open** Daily 7am–12am **Freeway** I-405,
CA-22W **Bus** 111, 112 (Long Beach) **Metro Rail** Blue line 801
to Pacific Coast Hwy (connection via bus or taxi)
The coffee house is wheelchair accessible

Although evenings and weekends can be busy, locals
enjoy this bohemian coffee house for its laidback
atmosphere during the weekdays and on nights when no
events are scheduled. Those who enjoy book browsing
are welcome to 'borrow' from any of the Library's
bookshelves while onsite.

Chango Coffee Shop

559 Echo Park Ave., LA 90026 ☎ (213) 977-9161
www.changoechopark.com **Open** Daily 7am–7pm **Parking**
Metered street parking **Freeway** CA-2, I/CA-110, US-101
Bus DASH Pico Union/Echo Park (LADOT) **Metro Rail** Red
line 802 to Vermont/Beverly (connection via bus or taxi)
The coffee house is wheelchair accessible

The gentle tapping of laptop keys and the intermittent hum
of an espresso machine are among the few ambient sounds
you're likely to hear in this small café, widely regarded as a
great neighborhood spot in which to work, read or study.
Livelier conversations may be heard outside, but the overall
atmosphere is conducive to relishing some quiet time.

Bricks & Scones

403 N. Larchmont Blvd., LA 90004 ☎ (323) 463-0811
www.bricksandscones.com **Open** Monday–Thursday
7.30am–9pm, Friday 7.30am–8pm, Saturday, Sunday
8am–8pm **Parking** Metered street parking **Freeway**
US-101 **Bus** 14, 37 (Metro Bus) **Metro Rail** Red line 802 to
Vermont/Beverly (connection via bus or taxi)
Patio and downstairs areas are wheelchair accessible

Bricks & Scones has a designated 'no-talking' room
upstairs—'the Study'—reserved for those who want to
read or work in silence. To enjoy a bit of quiet conversation
with your coffee, the downstairs room and semi-enclosed
outdoor courtyard offer plenty of comfortable seating areas.

Chado Tea Room

369 E. 1st St., LA 90012 ☎ (213) 258-2531 www.chadotea.com
Open Daily 11.30am–6pm **Parking** Paid lots, metered
street parking **Freeway** I-10, I/CA-110, US-101
Bus 30/330, 40 (Metro Bus), DASH A (LADOT)
Metro Rail Gold line 804 to Little Tokyo/Arts District
The tea room is wheelchair accessible

This tea room with attached fountain patio seating is
adjacent to the Japanese American National Museum
complex in Little Tokyo. More than 200 types of tea are on
the menu, along with appetizing sandwiches, soups, salads,
and tasty desserts.The friendly wait staff can offer tea
recommendations based on your palate and preferences.

Stories Books & Café

1716 W. Sunset Blvd., LA 90026 ☎ (213) 413-3733
www.storiesla.com **Open** Monday–Thursday 8am–9pm,
Friday 8am–10pm, Saturday 10am–10pm, Sunday 10am–
8pm **Parking** Free street parking **Freeway** CA-2, I/CA-110,
US-101 **Bus** 2, 4, 92, 200 (Metro Bus) DASH Pico Union/
Echo Park (LADOT) **Metro Rail** Red line 802 to Vermont/
Beverly (connection via bus or taxi)
The shop is wheelchair accessible

Local residents enjoy this neighborhood treasure for its
warm communal vibe where they can browse through a
thoughtful selection of books and enjoy baked goodies,
sandwiches, coffee, and tea in the adjacent café.

REDCAT Lounge

631 W. 2nd St., LA 90012 ☎ (213) 237-2800
www.redcat.org **Open** Tuesday–Friday 9am–8pm,
Saturday 12pm–8pm, Sunday 12pm–6pm **Parking** Paid
lots, metered street parking **Freeway** I-10, I/CA-110, US-
101 **Bus** 14/37 (Metro Bus), DASH A, B (LADOT)
Metro Rail Red/Purple line to Civic Center/Grand Park station
The lounge is wheelchair accessible

The elegant lobby and lounge inside the REDCAT arts
center can get crowded just before and after scheduled
performances; however, on a typical day, the lounge is a
perfectly lovely urban hideaway where one can enjoy a glass
of wine or an espresso in a calm, peaceful space.

Fix Coffee

2100 Echo Park Ave., LA 90026 ☎ (323) 284-8962
www.fixcoffeeco.com **Open** Daily 7am–7pm **Parking** Free
in lot, free street parking **Freeway** CA-2, I/CA-110, US-101
Bus DASH Pico Union/Echo Park (LADOT) **Metro Rail** Red
line 802 to Vermont/Beverly (connection via bus or taxi)
The shop is wheelchair accessible

The owner of this über cool coffee shop, Marc Gallucci, be-
lieves that 'coffee should matter,' but he also values community and connection, and has therefore created a welcoming
space where these three Cs can coexist in harmony. In addition to inside tables, a spacious covered patio offers ample
seating and welcomes guests with canine companions.

Café Gratitude (DTLA)

300 S. Santa Fe Ave., LA 90013 ☎ (213) 929-5580
www.cafegratitude.com **Open** Daily 8am–10pm
Parking Free in lot **Freeway** I-10, I/CA-110, US-101
Bus 30/330 (Metro Bus), DASH A (LADOT) **Metro Rail** Gold line 804 to Pico/Aliso
The café is wheelchair accessible

Everything on the menu at this vegan café is 100% organic and freshly prepared—no cans, no boxes, no frozen foods. Selections run a wide range, from mixed salads, sandwiches, and wraps to a variety of gourmet entrees. (If you try just one thing on the menu, make it the 'Warm-Hearted': grilled polenta with pumpkin seed cilantro pesto—yum!) Even better than its delicious foods are the creeds of Café Gratitude's noble and inspiring Mission, among them: sourcing foods locally; supporting sustainability and environmentally friendly practices; and encouraging people to be generous, grateful, and loving. Make sure to ask for the Question of the Day, which always encourages mindfulness with a positive view toward a greater collective consciousness.

Mignon Food + Wine

128 E. 6th St., LA 90014 ☎ (213) 489-0131
www.mignonla.com
Open Monday–Sunday 6pm–midnight
Parking Paid lots, metered street parking
Freeway I-10, I/CA-110, US-101
Bus 18, 53, 62 (Metro Bus), 720 (LADOT)
Metro Rail Red line 802/Purple line 805 to
Pershing Square
Outside patio is wheelchair accessible

If you're looking for a warm, cozy establishment
that caters to a more sophisticated crowd,
look no further than Mignon Food + Wine in
downtown's artsy Historic Core. This small
U-shaped wine bar seats about a dozen people
at a time and caters to those who enjoy elegant
French cuisine and a discerning wine list.
Charcuterie, cheese, and bread boards, small
plates, and mouth-watering entrees are offered
at reasonable prices by informed staff who can
suggest appropriate wine and food pairings, as
well as speak with authority to the distinctions of
each bottle on the list.

Literati Café
12081 Wilshire Blvd., LA 90025 ☎ (310) 231-7484
www.literaticafe.com
Open Monday-Friday 7am–11pm, Saturday, Sunday 8am–11pm
Parking Valet parking, metered street parking
Freeway I-405 **Bus** 20 (Metro Bus), Big Blue Bus Route 2 (Santa Monica)
Metro Rail Expo line 806 to Culver City (will require connection via bus or taxi)
The café is wheelchair accessible

Like a home away from home, Literati Café is one of those places that LA's West Siders frequent to enjoy a leisurely meal or to while away the hours with a cup of organic coffee and a newspaper, book, or crossword puzzle. This homey rustic space creates a welcoming environment, while an enclosed garden patio with large potted plants, comfy seating, and an ivy-covered trellis invites guests to take flight from the chaos of the city and enjoy a breather in tranquility.

Plant Food and Wine

1009 Abbot Kinney Blvd., Venice 90291 ☎ (310) 450-1009
matthewkenneycuisine.com/hospitality/plant-food-and-wine
Open Monday–Friday 11am–10pm, Saturday, Sunday
10am–10pm **Parking** Metered street parking **Freeway** I-10,
I-405, CA-90 **Bus** 33, 733 (Metro Bus) **Metro Rail** Expo line
806 to Culver City (connection via bus or taxi)
The restaurant is wheelchair accessible

This delightful restaurant serves up fresh, seasonal
plant-based cuisine and an organic wine list. Working
with locally sourced ingredients, vegetables, house-
made cheeses, seeds, grains, and legumes, each plated
appetizer and entrée is a work of culinary art in itself.

Piccolo Venice

5 Dudley Ave., Venice 90291 ☎ (310) 314-3222
www.piccolovenice.com **Open** Sunday–Thursday 5.30pm–
10.30pm, Friday, Saturday 5.30pm–11.30pm **Parking** Valet
parking, paid lots **Freeway** I-10, I-405, CA-90 **Bus** 33 (Metro
Bus), Big Blue Bus Route 1 (Santa Monica) **Metro Rail** Expo
line 806 to Culver City (connection via bus or taxi)
The restaurant is wheelchair accessible

Situated on a tiny Venice Beach cul-de-sac, this Zagat-
rated restaurant serves up authentic Italian cuisine, with an
exquisite menu by renowned chef Bobo Ivan. Be sure to ask
for a seat outside, where the sound of the surf and views of
the beach further enrich this magical dining experience.

Small shops and boutiques

Spring Arts Collective
inside the Spring Arts Tower
453 S. Spring St., Mezzanine, LA 90013
www.springarts.org
Open Wednesday–Saturday 11am–6pm, Sunday 1pm–6pm,
and by appointment (artists set their own hours)
Parking Metered street parking, paid lots
Freeway I-10, I/CA-110, US-101
Bus 14, 37, 70, 71, 76, 78, 79, 378 (Metro Bus)
Metro Rail Red line 802/ Purple line 805 to Pershing Square
The shops and galleries are wheelchair accessible

The Spring Arts Collective features the shops and galleries
of five LA artists, each with a distinctive aesthetic. Located
on the mezzanine of the Spring Arts Tower, an open gallery
leads first to installation artist and 'thingmaker' David
Lovejoy, who uses found objects, mechanical parts, and
vintage bric-a-brac to handcraft art that speaks to depth and
hidden meaning (lovejoyart.com). Fans of mixed media will
love Liz Huston's Studio Shoppe: an exquisite jewel-toned
space where Liz's evocative surrealist art and handmade
trinkets mingle against a backdrop of Victoriana, Old-World
apothecary, and a dash of Baroque (lizhuston.com). And
discovery, connection, and community are the threads woven
into Jena Priebe's space, FOLD Gallery & Nostalgia Shop.
Devoted entirely to the works of local artists, 'it's a place
where people can connect to each other while connecting
to the environment,' says Jena (folddtla.com). The artwork
of Dove Biscuit Studio (dovebiscuitstudio.com) and Andrea
Bogdan's Studio (andreabogdan.com) are also not to be
missed in this amazing creative space.

Gather DTLA

inside the Spring Arts Tower
453 S. Spring St., M1, LA 90013
☎ (213) 908-2656
www.togatherdtla.com
Open Monday, Tuesday, Thursday, Friday 11am–4pm, Wednesday, Saturday, Sunday 11am-7pm
Parking Metered street parking, paid lots
Freeway I-10, I/CA-110, US-101
Bus 14, 37, 70, 71, 76, 78, 79, 378 (Metro Bus)
Metro Rail Red line 802/ Purple line 805 to Pershing Square
The shop is wheelchair accessible

Knitting, crochet, spinning, and weaving enthusiasts will find respite in this homespun rustic space where locally- and U.S.-made, fair-trade, and eco-friendly yarn, fibers, needles, and supplies line the walls alongside beautifully handcrafted pieces. Experienced and patient instructors in this 'knitty nook in the city' teach a range of small group classes and offer private lessons for all levels of artisan; additionally, free Sunday Socials from 4pm–8pm invite 'yarnistas' to bring their projects and work alongside a friendly community of fiber aficionados.

Cookbook Los Angeles

1549 Echo Park Ave., LA 90026 ☎ (213) 250-1900
www.cookbookla.com **Open** Daily 9am–8pm **Parking** Free
street parking **Freeway** CA-2, I/CA-110, US-101 **Bus** DASH
Pico Union/Echo Park (LADOT) **Metro Rail** Red line 802 to
Vermont/Beverly (connection via bus or taxi)
The shop is not wheelchair accessible

This delightful neighborhood grocer enjoys small-town
charm like few locations in LA's urban mass. With its
variety of responsibly grown produce and artisanal meats,
cheeses, breads, and other freshly prepared foods, and
a small selection of cookbooks, gastronomes won't be
wanting for much in this quaint community market.

Blue Rooster Art Supplies

1718 N. Vermont Ave., LA 90027 ☎ (323) 661-9471
www.blueroosterartsupplies.com
Open Monday–Saturday 10am–8pm, Sunday 10am–7pm
Parking Paid lots, metered street parking **Freeway** US-101
Bus 180/181 (Metro Bus); DASH Hollywood (LADOT)
Metro Rail Red line 802 to Vermont/Sunset
The shop is not wheelchair accessible

'Wake Up, Make Something' is the tenet of this
independently owned Los Feliz art supplies store.
Managed by friendly and knowledgeable artists, the shop
carries a range of supplies across all media, while its
sister location in Atwater Village hosts select classes.

Silverlake Farmer's Market

3700 Sunset Blvd., LA 90026 ☎ (213) 484-4002
Open Tuesday 2pm–7.30pm, Saturday 9am–1pm
Parking Metered street parking
Freeway US-101 **Bus** 2, 4 (Metro Bus)
Metro Rail Red line 802 to Vermont/Beverly (connection via bus or taxi)
The market is wheelchair accessible, though some walkways are narrow

This outdoor venue accommodates a small number of vendors whose wares include vintage clothing, used books, organic produce, and packaged artisanal foods, alongside stalls that sell freshly prepared tamales, crêpes, and other delectable delights. Merchants are friendly, and the food vendors are known to offer free samples as a means of enticing passersby.

Tumbleweed and Dandelion

1502 Abbot Kinney Blvd., LA 90291 ☎ (310) 450-4310
www.tumbleweedanddandelion.com
Open Daily 10am–7pm
Parking Metered street parking **Freeway** I-10, I-405, CA-90 **Bus** 33, 733 (Metro Bus)
Metro Rail Expo line 806 to Culver City (connection via bus or taxi)
The shop is not wheelchair accessible

Beach bungalow, cottage, and French country design come together in this home-décor, antiques, and vintage shop. Staff are friendly, and customers are sure to find a treasure among the shop's selection of indoor and outdoor furnishings, linens, fabrics, decorative items, and garden statuary and accessories. Look for reclaimed pieces with distressed and worn patinas to add a bit of unique character to your home. Inquire within for interior design services and expertise in transforming your home into a beautiful haven.

San Antonio Winery

737 Lamar St., LA 90031 ☎ (323) 223-1401
www.sanantoniowinery.com
Open Sunday–Thursday 9am–7pm, Friday,
Saturday 9am–8pm
Parking Free in lot, free street parking
Freeway I-10, I/CA-110, US-101
Bus 76 (Metro Bus); DASH Lincoln Heights/
Chinatown (LADOT)
Metro Rail Gold line 804 to Chinatown
The winery is wheelchair accessible

At nearly 100 years old, the San Antonio Winery
still occupies its original downtown location.
Founded by Italian immigrant Santo Cambianica,
the historical winery managed to survive through
the bedlam of the Great Depression, Prohibition,
and World War II. In 1956, the business passed to
Cambianica's nephew, Stefano Riboli, and is still
owned and operated by the Riboli family today.
A tasting room, wine store, restaurant, and gift
shop are all on the premises, and wine tours are
complementary and offered daily on the hour.
For the most intimate experience, it's best to visit
during the week.

Piccolo Flowers

3200 E. Broadway, Long Beach 90803 ☎ (562) 434-1979
www.piccoloflowers.com
Open Monday–Saturday 10am–6pm
Parking Free street parking **Freeway** I-405, CA-22W
Bus 111, 112 (Long Beach) **Metro Rail** Blue line 801 to Pacific Coast Hwy (connection via bus or taxi)
The shop is wheelchair accessible

This locally owned corner flower shop has been serving the residents of Long Beach and the surrounding communities for more than 20 years. With blooms for every occasion, as well as custom arrangements, plants, and gift baskets, the shop's friendly proprietors, Vincent and Michelle Tumeo, serve walk-in guests with the same level of attention as large-scale event clients; moreover, they enjoy getting to know their customers on a personal level.

TOMS Flagship Store

1344 Abbot Kinney Blvd., Venice 90291 ☎ (310) 314-9700
www.toms.com **Open** Monday–Friday 6am–8pm, Saturday 7am–9pm, Sunday 7am–8pm
Parking Metered street parking **Freeway** I-10, I-405, CA-90 **Bus** 33, 733 (Metro Bus)
Metro Rail Expo line 806 to Culver City (will require connection via bus or taxi)
The store is wheelchair accessible

Ten years ago, TOMS started with a single mission: to give shoes to children in need. What began as a noble endeavor has since evolved into a worldwide enterprise. To date, TOMS has provided more than 45 million pairs of new shoes to children through its One for One® program, which helps a person in need every time a consumer makes a purchase. Today TOMS carries apparel, accessories, and a coffee line, the purchases of which go to support, among other things, clean-water, sight, and safer-birth programs. One-part retail shop, one-part coffeehouse, TOMS flagship store encourages community interaction with its indoor and outdoor gathering spaces, where people can enjoy conversation over a cup of coffee. The shop is busiest on the weekends; however, weekday mornings are comparatively relaxed.

The Wine Crush

131 E. Broadway, Long Beach 90803 ☎ (562) 438-9463
www.thewinecrush.com **Open** Tuesday, Wednesday 12pm–7pm, Thursday–Saturday 12pm–9pm, Sunday 12pm–6pm, closed Monday **Parking** Free street parking **Freeway** I-405, CA-22W **Bus** 111, 112 (Long Beach)
Metro Rail Blue line 801 to Pacific Coast Hwy (connection via bus or taxi)
The building is wheelchair accessible

Those looking for their next great bottle of wine can bet they'll find it in this small, unpretentious shop. Now in its 11th year, the store's knowledgeable buyers taste thousands of wines yearly to find the best bottles from regions around the world. An intimate tasting room makes for a more personal experience, with friendly staff who will gladly make recommendations to help tasters further develop their palates. A charming courtyard just outside contains a fire pit, umbrella-covered tables, and chairs where guests can enjoy a bottle and quiet conversation. Miniature white globe lights create a romantic ambience in the evenings; however, the shop frequently hosts events during the weekend, so call ahead to check the schedule if you aren't in the mood for a larger crowd.

Sculpture Gardens

1029½ Abbot Kinney Blvd., Venice 90291 ☎ (310) 399-0321
www.sculpture-gardens.com **Open** Tuesday–Sunday 12pm–4pm
Parking Metered street parking **Freeway** I-10, I-405, CA-90 **Bus** 33, 733 (Metro Bus)
Metro Rail Expo line 806 to Culver City (connection via bus or taxi)
The store is not wheelchair accessible

This imaginative, eclectic community nursery has been serving the residents of Venice for nearly 50 years. Much more than a plant shop, visitors enter through a narrow enclosed walkway and will undoubtedly feel as though they've been transported to a secret garden when they emerge on the other side. Sculpture, statuary, and wind chimes surround a small koi pond shaded by trees and flowering shrubs, including *Melaleuca Nesophila,* a 45-year-old myrtle with a pink puff-like bloom. A four-citrus-producing tree, more than 35 types of abutilon, cacti, succulents, orchids, and ornamentals are just a few of this shop's offerings, with new flora added regularly. Make sure to chat with the staff who enjoy talking about the store's unique history.

Urban Americana

1345 Coronado Ave., Long Beach 90804 ☎ (562) 494-7300
www.urbanamericana.com **Open** Daily 10am–6pm
Parking Free in lot **Freeway** I-405, CA-22W
Bus 45 (Long Beach) **Metro Rail** Blue line 801 to Pacific
Coast Hwy (connection via bus or taxi)
The building is wheelchair accessible

This antique and design collective features aisle after
aisle of one-of-a-kind vintage wares. Mid-century modern
furnishings, lighting, and signage share space alongside
unique folk art, pottery, and other collectibles. An outdoor
nursery filled with arrangements of aloe, agave, succulents,
and other shrubs add an unexpected yet welcome touch.

Flax Pen to Paper

1078 Gayley Ave., LA 90024 ☎ (310) 208-3529
www.flaxpentopaper.com **Open** Tuesday–Friday 10am–7pm,
Saturday 10am–5.30pm **Parking** Paid lots, metered street
parking **Freeway** I-405 **Bus** 6, 6R, 20, 234 (Metro Bus); Big
Blue Bus Routes 1, 2, 3M, 8, 12 (Santa Monica) **Metro Rail**
Expo line 806 to Culver City (connection via bus or taxi)
The shop is wheelchair accessible

Pen and paper reign supreme here and customers will want
to disconnect their digital devices to explore shelves filled with
journals, notebooks, and fine stationery. The soothing sounds
of cello music or jazz might play lightly in the background, but
won't disturb your experience in this scribe's heaven.

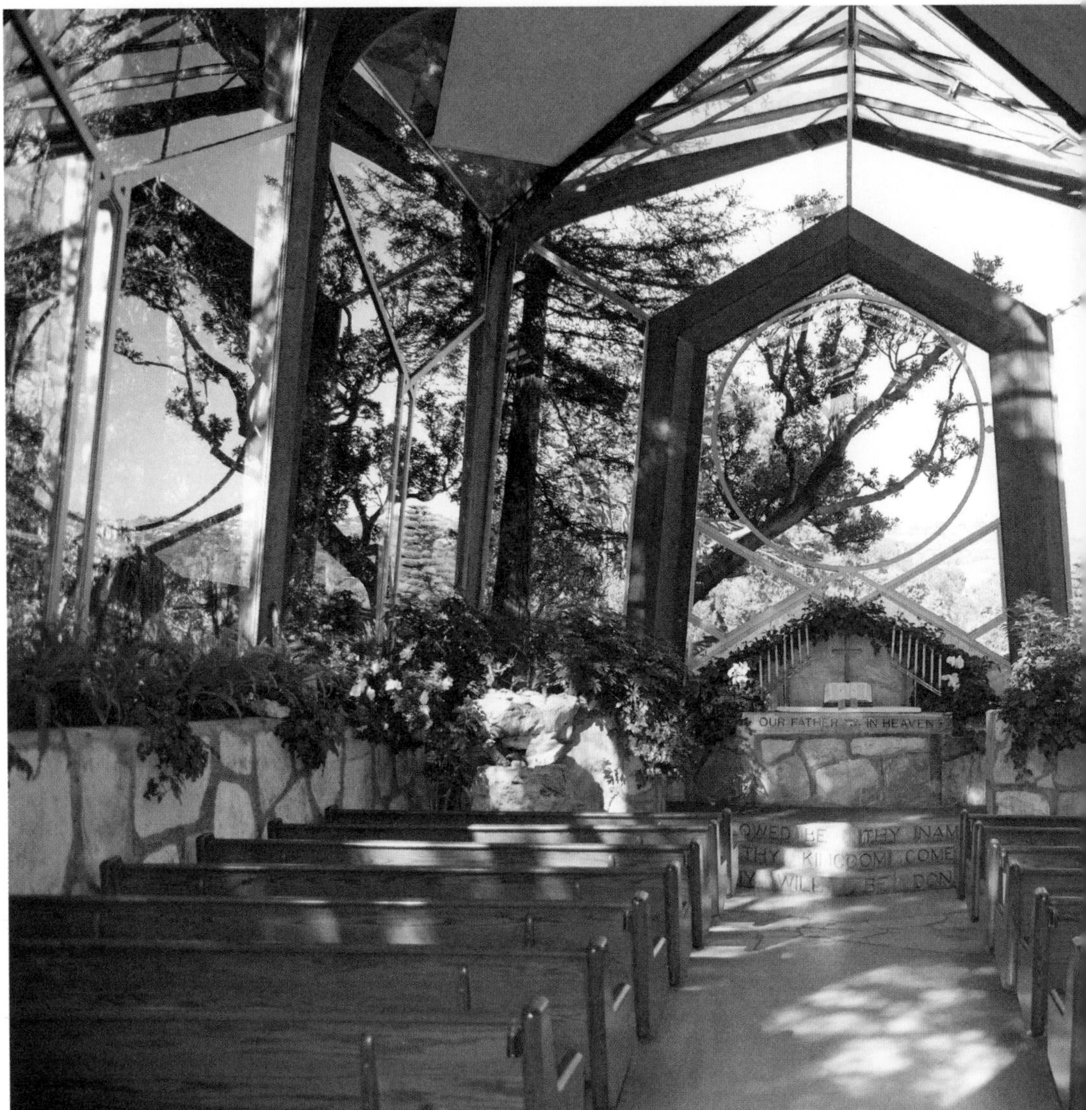
OUR FATHER
IN HEAVEN

Places to sit and walk

Wayfarers Chapel

5755 Palos Verdes Drive South, Rancho Palos Verdes 90275
☎ (310) 377-1650
Free www.wayfarerschapel.org
Open Grounds: daily 9am–5pm; visitors center: daily 10am–5pm
Parking Free in lot **Freeway** I/CA-110
Bus 344 (Metro Bus); Orange, Gold, Blue, 225, 226 (Palos Verdes Peninsula Transit)
Metro Rail Green line 803 to Harbor Freeway station (connection via bus or taxi)
The chapel is wheelchair accessible; there are some inclines

Sweeping ocean vistas, stunning gardens, brick and stone pathways, and a beautiful fountain naturally inspire reverence and quiet reflection at the Wayfarers Chapel. The exquisite glass-framed chapel encased by redwood trees is an example of Organic Architecture wherein the 'trees are the forms and the space within the forms is sacred space.' Designed by Lloyd Wright, son of renowned architect Frank Lloyd Wright, the Chapel hosts worship services on Sundays and at select times of the year; however, visitors are welcome to enjoy this tranquil space and its grounds year-round. The idea to create a chapel for wayfarers was first championed in the 1920s by Elizabeth Schellenberg, a resident of the Palos Verdes Peninsula and a member of the freethinking Swedenborgian Church. After a series of delays, the structure was completed in 1951 and dedicated to 18th-century scientist and theologian Emanuel Swedenborg, the church's progressive founder. Today people from all over the world come to visit this quiet, sacred place for its calm and tranquil atmosphere.

Mission San Juan Capistrano

26801 Ortega Hwy, San Juan Capistrano 92675
☎ (949) 234-1300
$ (free for children under 3)
www.missionsjc.com
Open Daily 9am–5pm. Check website for dates
and times of guided tours
Parking Paid lots **Freeway** I-5
Bus 91 (Orange County Transportation)
Metro Link Orange County line / Inland
Empire-Orange County line to San Juan
Capistrano Metrolink Station
Most of the grounds are wheelchair accessible

While not officially located in Los Angeles
County, the Mission San Juan Capistrano is a
Southern California landmark with a unique
history deserving of the trip into coastal south
Orange County. Founded by Father Serra on
November 1, 1776, the mission was established—
as were all California missions—to convert
Native Americans to Christianity and the
European way of life. While the Mission's history
includes numerous tales of lore, one true story
is the 'Miracle of the Swallows.' Every year on
March 19th, the swallows end their migration
from South America at the Mission to rebuild
their nests in the ruins of the Great Stone
Church, which was destroyed in an earthquake
in 1812. The diminutive birds stay through the
summer until October 23rd when they start
their winter migration back to their home in
Argentina. The Mission bell rings daily at 9am
in tribute to Father Serra, and the Swallows
Walk & Talk tour is offered daily at 1pm. Chapel,
garden, and guided tours are also offered at
various times.

Bradbury Building

304 S. Broadway, LA 90013 ☎ (213) 626-1893
Free www.laconservancy.org/locations/
bradbury-building
Open Daily during normal business hours
Parking Paid in lots, metered street parking
Freeway I-10, I/CA-110, US-101 **Bus** 2, 4, 30/330,
40, 45, 745 (Metro Bus) **Metro Rail** Red line 802/
Purple line 805 to Pershing Square
The building is wheelchair accessible

Those who appreciate turn-of-the-century
craftsmanship will want to stop in to the
Bradbury Building, an architectural jewel in
downtown LA. Inside the c. 1893 Romanesque
edifice, expansive skylights fill the main court
with natural light, while open corridors with
cast-iron and polished-wood railings run the
length of the perimeter on the floors above.
Intricately carved woodwork, dentil molding,
exposed brick, marble staircases, and paneled
ceilings are revealing of the structure's Victorian
roots, while the original mail slots and open-
cage lifts are beautiful in their own right. As the
building is home to professional offices, only the
first floor and first stair landing are open to the
public; however, the space is most enjoyable on
the weekends anyway when there is less foot
traffic. Bonus points go to the bronze Charlie
Chaplin statue seated on a bench inside a
vestibule, which makes for a great photo-op.

Ballona Lagoon Marine Preserve
Marquesas Way and Via Dolce, Marina Del Rey, 90292 **Free**
Parking Free and metered street parking **Freeway** I-10, I-405, CA-90 **Bus** 108, 358 (Metro Bus)
Metro Rail Expo line 806 to Culver City (connection via bus or taxi)
The paved walkway along Via Marina at Pacific Ave. is wheelchair accessible

Also known as the Pacific Flyway, this travel stop for hundreds of species of bird is located along the 2,000-mile migration route between Alaska and Latin America. As a scenic walk, it is one of LA's best-kept secrets and far less congested than the Venice Canals nearby. Numerous plants and marine life inhabit this protected inlet, making it particularly interesting to those concerned with marine ecosystems. Start at Marquesas Way and Via Dolce, heading south along the path until it ends at Via Marina; head west to Pacific Ave, making sure to stop along the paved walkway directly across the street to take in the views of the Marina Del Rey Harbor channel where you're sure to see a sailboat or two cruise through. Continue north up Pacific Avenue until you get to Lighthouse Street. Cross the canal and head north around the bend to complete the loop back up to the starting point.

PacMutual Building

523 W. 6th St., LA 90014
Free www.pacmutualdtla.com
Open Daily during normal business hours
Parking Paid lots, metered street parking
Freeway I-10, I/CA-110, US-101
Bus 2, 4, 30/330, 40,
45, 745 (Metro Bus)
Metro Rail Red line 802/Purple line 805 to
Pershing Square
The building is wheelchair accessible

Registered as City of Los Angeles Historical-
Cultural Monument No. 398, the Beaux-
Arts-style PacMutual Building in downtown
consists of three connected historically relevant
structures: the Sentry Building (c. 1921), the
Clock Building (c. 1908), and the Carriage House
(c. 1926). Weekends are a great time to pop into
the Sentry Building for a glimpse of its ornate
barrel-vaulted ceiling; elegant Italian Tavernelle
marble staircases, pillars, and balustrades; and
polished tile floors. Limited seating is available
for a few minutes' repose to fully admire the
architectural details. Outside, a small open-air
patio at 507 W. 6th Street, between the Sentry
Building and the Clock Building, is a pleasant
spot to enjoy a quick bite.

Naples Canals

at The Toledo and Rivo Alto Canal, Long Beach 90803 **Free**
Parking Free and metered street parking
Freeway I-405, CA-22W **Bus** 121, 131 (Long Beach)
Metro Rail Blue line 801 to Pacific Coast Hwy (connection via bus or taxi)
Canal bridges are wheelchair accessible via paved sidewalks; however, several steps leading to the canal pathways make accessibility difficult

Formed in the early 20th century by land developer Arthur M. Parsons, the Naples Canals mark the division of three separate islands that comprise this quiet waterfront community on Alamitos Bay. Five bridges cross the canals at different points, and the pathways are open to the public (and their leashed canine companions), who are sure to spot kayakers, paddle boarders, and boaters taking quiet laps around the bay. After Thanksgiving and through the New Year, residents start bedecking their homes and boats secured in the slips with colorful, twinkly lights, making this self-guided walking tour even more charming when the sun goes down.

Watts Towers

1761 E. 107th St., LA 90002 ☎ (213) 847-4646
Free www.wattstowers.org **Open** Guided tours: Thursday,
Friday, Saturday 10.30am–3pm, Sunday 12.30pm–3pm
Parking Free street parking **Freeway** I-105,
I/CA-110 **Bus** 117, 612 (Metro Bus) **Metro Rail** Metro Blue Line
801 to 103rd Street/Watts Towers
The location is wheelchair accessible

This extraordinary public art installation is the work of Simon
'Sam' Rodia. It took 33 years to complete: 17 steeple-like
circular sculptures, which he crafted from steel and mortar
using ordinary construction tools, and then emblazoned with
multi-colored pieces of tile, glass, pottery, and seashells.

Avon-Baxter Stairs

Baxter St. and Avon St., LA 90026
Open All day, every day **Freeway** US-101 **Bus** DASH Pico
Union/Echo Park (LADOT) **Metro Rail** Red line 802 to
Vermont/Beverly (connection via bus or taxi)
The location is not wheelchair accessible

With more than 230 steps to mount, ascending this incline
might be a bit challenging; however, the views of the Echo
Park and Silverlake neighborhoods once you reach the top
are unsurpassed. Just east of the summit are the sloping
hills of Elysian Park. If you head north, you'll run into Chavez
Ravine Road, which leads right into the Chavez Ravine
Arboretum—another quiet and scenic spot to take a break.

Hollywood Forever Cemetery

6000 Santa Monica Blvd., Hollywood 90038
☎ (323) 469-1181
Free www.hollywoodforever.com
Open Grounds open daily, 8am–5pm
Freeway US-101 **Bus** 4 (Metro Bus), DASH
Hollywood-Wilshire (LADOT)
Metro Rail Red line 802 to Hollywood/Vine
Pathways around the grounds are wheelchair accessible

This cultural landmark is the final resting place of some of Hollywood's biggest names, including Cecil B. DeMille, Jayne Mansfield, Tyrone Power, Rudolph Valentino, and countless other actors, writers, directors, and musicians. Founded in 1899, Hollywood Forever is a functioning funeral home and cemetery. Its immaculate grounds are covered in verdant lawns, palm trees, gardens, fountains, and statuary. The beautifully constructed Lake Island Mausoleum is the resting place of William Clark Jr., founder of the Los Angeles Philharmonic Orchestra, while actor Douglas Fairbanks Jr. lays next to his equally famous father, Douglas Fairbanks Sr., in a marble tomb and monument at the head of a rectangular well. Maps are available for those interested in navigating these grounds that pay tribute to Hollywood royalty, but even without a guide, one can enjoy this quiet spot for its beauty alone.

Delta Street Stairs

Delta St. and Echo Park Ave., LA 90026
Open All day, every day
Freeway US-101
Bus DASH Pico Union/Echo Park (LADOT)
Metro Rail Red line 802 to Vermont/Beverly
(connection via bus or taxi)
The location is not wheelchair accessible

Delta Street ends in a cul-de-sac where 125
steps lead up to Lucretia Avenue. Once you
make it to the top, make a quick left to grab
the 69 steps that lead down to Grafton Street.
Once on Grafton, hang a left to head back to
Echo Park Avenue. Another left gets you back
to Delta where you started. While not a very
long distance, a brisk walk along this quiet
neighborhood route is enough to get your
heart pumping.

Christian Science Reading Room

Third Church of Christ, Scientist
730 S. Hope St., LA 90017 ☎ (213) 622-3639
www.christiansciencereadingroom.info
Open By appointment and before/after regular services: Sunday 11am, Wednesday 7pm
Parking Paid lots, metered street parking **Freeway** I-10, I/CA-110, US-101 **Bus** 66, 81 (Metro Bus)
Metro Rail Blue line 801/Red line 802/Purple line 805/Expo line 806 to 7th Street/Metro Center
The building is wheelchair accessible

The peace, reverence, and inclusivity of the Christian Science community make visiting a reading room or attending a service a unique and uplifting experience for those of all backgrounds. Based on the tenet of healing through prayer, this faith-based kinship invites those who are seeking quiet time in spiritual contemplation and Biblical study to peruse the many materials available in their reading rooms. Staff are generally onsite and available to discuss the Christian Science faith; however, individuals may also choose to read and study materials undisturbed.

Korean Bell of Friendship and Bell Pavilion

at Angels Gate Park, 3601 Gaffey St., San Pedro 90731 ☎ (310) 548-7705
Free www.sanpedro.com/sp_point/korenbel.htm
Open 10am–6pm (subject to close without notice) **Parking** Free in lot
Freeway I/CA-110 **Bus** 246 (Metro Bus) **Metro Rail** Green line 803 to Harbor Freeway station (connection via bus or taxi)
The location is wheelchair accessible

Modeled after the centuries-old Divine Bell of King Seongdeok the Great, on exhibit in the Gyeongju National Museum, the Korean government commissioned the Friendship Bell especially for the people of Los Angeles. Donated in 1976 to commemorate the U.S. bicentennial, honor Korean War veterans, and celebrate friendship between the two nations, the 17-ton bell was crafted from copper, tin, gold, nickel, lead, and phosphorous in Korea and shipped to the U.S. An intricate, brilliantly colored pavilion provides shelter for the ornate bell, which sits atop a hill overlooking the Pacific Ocean and the Los Angeles Harbor. While the bell is only rung four times a year on Independence Day, Korean Independence Day, New Year's Eve, and in September to observe Constitution Week, the grounds are open year round for visitors to see the bell up close.

Los Angeles City Hall

200 N Spring St., LA 90012 ☎ (213) 978-1995
Free (docent-led tours require advanced reservations)
www.lacity.org
Open Monday–Friday 10am–5pm
Parking Paid lots, metered street parking
Freeway I-10, I/CA-110, US-101 **Bus** 28, 33, 70, 71, 76, 78/79/378, 83, 92, 96, 487/489, 493, 495, 497, 498, 499, 699 (Metro Bus); DASH A, B, D (LADOT)
Metro Rail Red line 802/Purple line 805 to Civic Center/Grand Park
The building is wheelchair accessible

Built in 1928, the City Hall building is Los Angeles personified. It's not the tallest building downtown (it lost that distinction in the 1960s) nor is it the most impressive, but it is an emblem of the city's rich and storied history. While the builders made no definitive claim as to the structure's architectural style, its tower and interior design are reminiscent of Art Deco. A rotunda, coved ceilings, and columns are among the beautiful interior details on the 27th floor, where an observation deck offers the most stunning views of the city skyline and beyond. Docent-led tours are offered daily and include the Rotunda, City Council Chambers, the Hall of Mayors, and the Mayor's gifts. Self-guided tour materials are also available.

Cove-Alvarado Stairs

2100 W. Cove Ave., LA 90039
Open All day, every day
Freeway I-5, CA-2 **Bus** 603 (Metro Bus)
Metro Link 91 Line, Antelope Valley, Orange
County, San Bernardino
Location is not wheelchair accessible

Just two steps shy of 200, this tree-lined
stairway is tucked into a hilly residential
area that offers pretty views of the Silverlake
Reservoir and surrounding community below.
The top of the stairs begins at 2100 W. Cove
Avenue, but for a more vigorous workout, start
your walk at the bottom (2130 W. Cove Ave.) and
climb up. Multiple landings allow walkers to
stop and catch their breath along the way. To
continue the workout once at the peak, head
south to Baxter Street; then turn east and
continue walking until you reach the highest
point at Lemoyne Street. The Baxter Street
hills are among the steepest through this quiet
neighborhood, and on a clear day you can see
the Hollywood Sign and Griffith Observatory in
the hills to the west.

Quiet drives

Mulholland Drive, Los Angeles
Suggested route Start Mulholland Dr. at I-405; drive east, ending at Cahuenga Blvd. West
Distance Approx. 12 miles one way

Mulholland Drive weaves its way through a string of canyons and the Hollywood Hills with a number of overlooks and photo-worthy vistas. Don't miss the Hollywood Bowl Overlook, which features spectacular views of the Hollywood sign and the sprawl of the city.

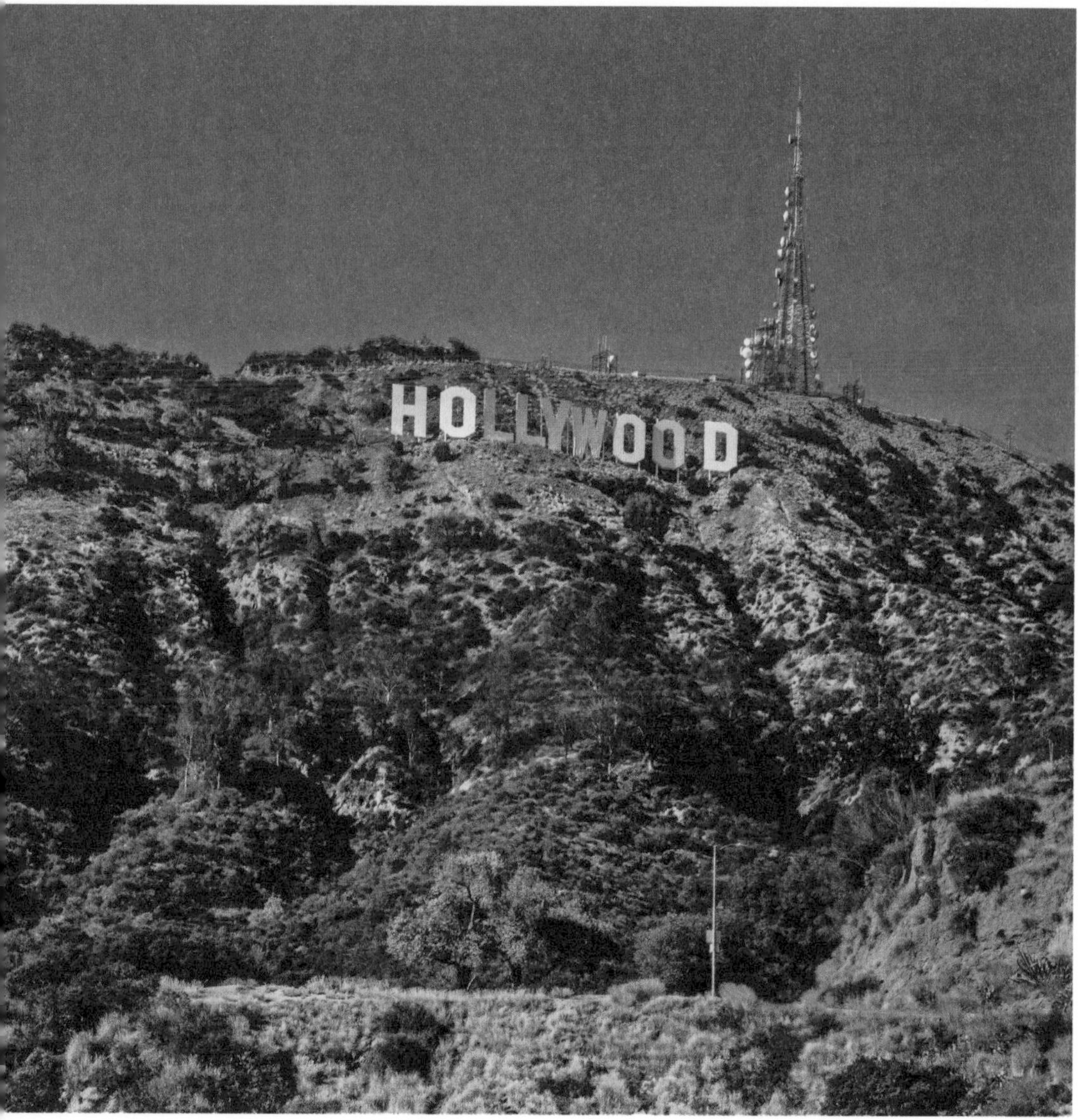
HOLLYWOOD

Mulholland Highway, Los Angeles
Suggested route Begin Mulholland Highway at
CA-23, head east and end at CA-27
Distance Approx. 17 miles one way

Not to be confused with Mulholland Drive,
Mulholland Highway bends its way through the
Santa Monica Mountains and Malibu Creek State
Park, with multiple points of interest along the
way. One of these spots is Paramount Ranch,
where numerous movies and TV series have
been filmed, dating back to 1927. Today the
ranch features a permanent 'western town'
set that is open to the public. This drive is best
taken during the week, as weekends tend to
attract tourists and motorcycle riders en masse.

Palos Verdes Drive, San Pedro to Rancho Palos Verdes

Suggested route Start at W. 25th St. in San Pedro; head north to Palos Verdes Drive South, continuing to Palos Verdes Drive West. Continue north on Palos Verdes Drive West to Paseo Lunado; head west following the road to Paseo Del Mar; end at Palos Verdes Estates Shoreline Preserve.
Distance Approx. 15 miles one way

One of the most scenic drives in Los Angeles County, this coastal route has many points of interest, including numerous parks and vehicle turnouts to take in the breathtaking views of the Pacific. Several recreational areas along this course make it easy to stop and enjoy an afternoon picnic and hike.

Elysian Park: Stadium Way to Angels Point Drive, Los Angeles

Suggested route From I-5, take Stadium Way south to Angels Point Rd.; continue to Grand View Dr. then to Park Row Dr.; head north to Solano Canyon Dr. Turn south to Academy Rd.; then west to Academy Dr.* back to Elysian Park Dr. where it meets again with Angels Point Drive. (*Note: This route crosses both Academy Road and Academy Drive.)
Distance Approx. 5 miles round trip

Those wishing to take a short leisurely drive will enjoy the sights along the gently winding roads through Chavez Ravine. Make sure to stop at the Angels Point overlook for unobstructed views of downtown LA.

Pacific Coast Highway (PCH), Pacific Palisades

Suggested route Start PCH at Temescal Canyon Rd., heading north. End at Las Posas Rd.
Distance Approx. 35 miles one way

The drive along this section of Pacific Coast Highway, or PCH, divides the Pacific Ocean from the Santa Monica Mountains, with no shortage of magnificent views to take in through Malibu. Stop at Point Mugu State Park where bluffs, canyons, and trails overlook the ocean. Better yet, take a walk down to the shore for a peaceful stroll along one of the small, quiet beaches along this route.

Angeles Crest Highway (CA-2), La Cañada Flintridge

Suggested route Start Angeles Crest Highway at Foothill Blvd. and take until it ends at CA-138.

Distance Approx. 65 miles one way

This exceedingly winding road cuts through the heart of Angeles National Forest. Blind corners and hairpin turns can make the road challenging, but cautious drivers will have no problem navigating the terrain. While there are a number of scenic spots along the way, this highway can also be thoroughly enjoyed from the car without stopping.

Latigo Canyon Road, Malibu

Suggested route Begin Latigo Canyon Rd. at Pacific Coast Highway; follow the road around to Kanan Dume Rd., head south back to Pacific Coast Highway.

Distance Approx. 15 miles round trip

This short drive on these twisting streets through Malibu treats roadsters to some stunning views of the coast, in addition to the hills and canyons of the Santa Monica Mountains. Wildflowers grow in abundance here and there are a few vehicle turnouts. This is a great drive on a clear day with the top down or the sunroof open.

Places to stay

The Langham Huntington Hotel & Spa

1401 South Oak Knoll Ave., Pasadena 91106
☎ (626) 568-3900
www.langhamhotels.com/en/the-langham/pasadena
Parking Paid lot
Freeway I-210, I-605
Bus 485 (Metro Bus)
Metro Rail Gold line 804 to Sierra Madre (connection via bus or taxi)
The hotel and spa are wheelchair accessible

Impeccably landscaped lawns, well-appointed rooms, traditional British afternoon tea, and gorgeous views of the San Gabriel Mountains are just some of the things guests can expect from a stay at this hotel. While the resort includes plenty of amenities to keep active people busy, it is perfect for those seeking a quiet, restful escape thanks to a selection of private-balcony rooms; acres of serene gardens, footpaths, and fountains; a day spa inspired by Traditional Chinese Medicine; and other quiet nooks and crannies throughout. Take some time to walk through the nearby residential San Marino neighborhood, which is one of the most scenic in Southern California. For the most relaxing experience, this location is best avoided during peak summer months.

Topanga Canyon Inn Bed & Breakfast

20310 Callon Dr., Topanga 90290 ☎ (310) 570-3791
www.topangacanyoninn.com
Parking Free onsite **Freeway** I-405, US-101
Some rooms and common areas are wheelchair accessible (call ahead to reserve parking and for complete details)

Nestled into the secluded hills of Topanga State Park, and well away from the sounds of passing traffic, this Mediterranean-style inn consists of two dwellings: the Casa Blanca and the Casa Rosa. Wherever guests stay, they can be assured a peaceful sojourn surrounded by magnificent mountain vistas, as well as the sounds and fragrances of nature just outside the door. Each cozy, cheerful room is inspired by a famous Hollywood couple, including Rhett & Scarlett, Bogey & Bacall, and Fred & Ginger, and most have beautiful canyon views. Owned and operated by Warren and Elena Roché, the Inn reflects a family's labor of love. Warren designed and built both structures himself; Elena's plein air paintings grace the Inn's walls; and the couple's five children help out in various capacities. Guests are welcomed and treated like family during their stay.

The Beverly Hills Hotel

9641 Sunset Blvd., Beverly Hills 90210 ☎ (310) 276-2251
www.dorchestercollection.com **Parking** Valet parking
Freeway I-405 **Bus** 2 (Metro Bus) **Metro Rail** Red line 802
to Vermont/Santa Monica (connection via bus or taxi)
The hotel is wheelchair accessible

Elizabeth Taylor, Marilyn Monroe, Marlene Dietrich, and
countless other celebrities have stayed at this iconic hotel,
which is why those seeking quiet—combined with a fair
amount of luxury—won't be disappointed. Private bungalows
offer the ultimate secluded experience, but if that's not in
the budget, the rooms and suites won't fail to satisfy with
comforts that include private patios, kitchens, and more.

Farmer's Daughter Hotel

115 S. Fairfax Ave., LA 90036 ☎ (323) 937-3930
www.farmersdaughterhotel.com **Parking** Paid lot
Freeway I-10, I-405 **Bus** 16/316, 217, 218 (Metro Bus), DASH
Fairfax (LADOT) **Metro Rail** Red line 802 to Vermont/Beverly
(connection via bus or taxi)
The hotel is wheelchair accessible

Mid-century modern meets country farmhouse with a
dash of kitsch at this quirky boutique hotel. It's close
to several of LA's tourist spots, but with rooms tranquil
enough to come back to after a long day of sightseeing.
The quietest rooms are away from the pool toward the
rear of the hotel, and summer can be busy.

The Bissell House Bed & Breakfast

201 Orange Grove Ave., South Pasadena 91030 ☎ (626) 441-3535
www.bissellhouse.com
Parking Free onsite
Freeway I/CA-110 **Bus** 176, 260 (Metro Bus)
Metro Rail Gold line 804 to South Pasadena
The building is not wheelchair accessible

For quiet repose in an enchanting neighborhood, guests will savor the delights of 19th-century charm in this historic home. Albert Einstein once dined here at the invitation of Anna Bissell McKay (daughter of vacuum magnate Melville Bissell), who owned the dwelling from 1902 to the 1950s. Built in 1887, the three-story Shingle-style Bed & Breakfast features eight beautifully furnished rooms with all of the comforts one needs to unwind. Complimentary breakfast, afternoon sweets, and a self-serve round-the-clock tea table are among the amenities, while the area itself is ideal for taking a relaxing stroll amid other beautifully restored historic homes.

Hotel Bel-Air

701 Stone Canyon Road, LA 90077 ☎ (310) 472-1211
www.dorchestercollection.com
Parking Valet parking
Freeway I-405 **Bus** 2, 2/302, 234 (Metro Bus, no direct access)
Metro Rail Red line 802 to Hollywood/Western (connection via bus or taxi)
The hotel is wheelchair accessible

If money is no object, you won't want to pass up the opportunity to spend some well-deserved quiet time in total opulence. Far above the sounds and distractions of the city, this beguiling escape is surrounded by quiet hilly roads and, just inside its boundary, acres of stunning, fragrant gardens. Swan Lake is an enticing area to enjoy a picnic on the lawn or simply take in the beautiful surroundings. Rooms are modern and sophisticated with a range of conveniences that make settling in for a relaxing stay all too easy.

Tuscali Mountain Inn Luxury Bed & Breakfast

1224 North Topanga Canyon Blvd., Topanga 90290 ☎ (310) 455-1828
www.tuscalimountaininn.com
Parking Free in lot **Freeway** I-405, US-101
Location is not wheelchair accessible

This 'little piece of Tuscany in Southern California' lives up to its reputation as a peaceful retreat tucked into the Santa Monica Mountains, well away from the congestion of town. With only two guest rooms—and private access to each—visitors are assured a worry-free, therapeutic getaway. Amenities include complimentary Wi-Fi, a cozy great room, and a romantic courtyard with fountain and exquisite vistas of the surrounding canyons. Evening hors d'oeuvres are offered and complimentary wines enjoyed. Hosts Bruce and Teresa Royer treat guests to delicious homemade breakfasts in the relaxed dining room.

Terranea Resort

6610 Palos Verdes Drive South, Rancho Palos Verdes 90275 ☎ (310) 265-2800
www.terranea.com
Parking Valet parking **Freeway** I/CA-110
Bus 344 (Metro Bus); Orange, Gold, Blue, 225, 226 (Palos Verdes Peninsula Transit)
Metro Rail Green line 803 to Harbor Freeway station (connection via bus or taxi)
The resort is wheelchair accessible

Situated atop a bluff overlooking the Pacific Ocean, this eco-conscious Mediterranean-style resort is large in size, but channels the intimate ambience of a boutique hotel thanks to its idyllic location and a design (and staff) that prizes guests' privacy and need for quiet relaxation. Visitors may choose from a bungalow, casita, villa, or standard room for their stay, all of which feature private balconies—most with ocean views. Secluded beach coves, tide pools, and hiking trails around the Palos Verdes Peninsula are easily accessible from the property, while a spa and oceanfront yoga and Pilates studio offer a standing invitation to decompress.

Acknowledgments

Thank you to Andrew Dunn and Nicki Davis for your time and patience, and for giving me the creative freedom to run with this project. Thanks to my dear friend Jickie Torres for allowing me to borrow your husband almost every weekend for six months straight—including on Valentine's Day—so that he could run around the city with me taking pretty pictures. Thanks to Mark Mendez for giving up almost every weekend for six months straight—including on Valentine's Day—to work with me, keeping me laughing the entire time (and showing no fear when those fits of laughter almost caused a car accident on more than one occasion.) Many thanks to Meghan O'Dell, Peter Macomber, Hadley Tomicki and Tatiana Arbogast, Karen Stretch Fletcher, Katy French, Amanda Tannen, Marianne Liggett, Breanna Vargas, and David Razo for your referrals and suggestions. Heartfelt thanks to all of the amazing shop owners and employees, who so generously gave of their time and ideas. And a very special thank you to Siobhan Wall, whose vision and mission to find peace and tranquility in the midst of chaotic city centers made this little book possible.

About the Author

Born and raised in Southern California, Rebecca Razo has been a writer and editor for more than 16 years, covering everything from art and literature to architecture, interior design, and holistic health. A former Los Angeles City employee for nearly a decade, Rebecca grew up in the LA suburbs and loves the city as much for its rich heritage as for its cultural, geographical, and artistic diversity. Visit www.rebeccarazo.com.

About the Photographer

Mark Mendez is a photographer, artist, and graphic designer who discovered the art of picture taking in high school, further developing his skills in college where he majored in Advertising Design and minored in Photography. Since then, Mark has shot for a number of multi-national magazines in addition to corporate product photography and privately commissioned projects. Visit www.markerarts.com.